trisha's table

trisha's table

MY FEEL-GOOD FAVORITES FOR A BALANCED LIFE

Trisha Yearwood

with Beth Yearwood Bernard

FOREWORD BY Garth Brooks

PHOTOGRAPHS BY BEN FINK

CLARKSON POTTER/PUBLISHERS
NEW YORK

Copyright © 2015 by Trisha Yearwood
Interior photographs copyright © 2015 by Ben Fink
Cover photograph copyright © 2015 by Perry Hagopian

Published in the United States by Clarkson Potter/Publishers, an
imprint of the Crown Publishing Group, a division of Penguin Random
House LLC, New York.
crownpublishing.com
clarksonpotter.com

CLARKSON POTTER is a trademark and POTTER with colophon is a
registered trademark of Penguin Random House LLC.

Originally published in hardcover in the United States by Clarkson
Potter/Publishers, an imprint of the Crown Publishing Group, a
division of Penguin Random House LLC, New York, in 2015.

All photographs are by Ben Fink with the exception of those appearing
on pages 5, 9, 20, 46, 52, 57, 70, 88, 91, 92, 96, 101, 118, 124, 158, 161,
164, 168, 181, 203, and 224, which are from the author's collection.

Library of Congress Cataloging-in-Publication Data
Yearwood, Trisha.
Trisha's table : my feel-good favorites for a balanced life / Trisha
Yearwood.
pages cm
1. Cooking, American—Southern style. I. Title.
TX715.2.S68Y433 2015
641.5975—dc23
2014029104

ISBN 978-1-5247-6094-6
Ebook ISBN 978-0-8041-8616-2

Printed in the United States of America

Book design by Rae Ann Spitzenberger
Cover design by Michael Nagin
Cover front photograph by Perry Hagopian

10 9 8 7 6 5 4 3 2 1

First Paperback Edition

We learned to cook, laugh, and love in all those years growing up around the Yearwood table. We shared life's triumphs and disappointments over many a suppertime, and we learned the value of that simple daily ritual— the family meal. No matter what our days were like, we gathered for supper every night. As we got older we would find ourselves sitting at the table long after the meal was finished, just talking and laughing. The family meal brought us together, and it's time that we will cherish forever. This book is dedicated to our parents, Jack and Gwen Yearwood, who were the best teachers any child could hope for. Thank you for sharing your passion for food with us, and for teaching us the importance of family. You fed us body, heart, and soul. No matter what we do or where our lives take us, we are most proud and grateful to be your daughters.

Love,

Beth & Patricia

Angel Hair Pasta with
Avocado Pesto (page 132)

contents

foreword

Miss Yearwood and I have known each other for twenty-five years. We both moved to Nashville in the mid-1980s, we both signed record deals at the turn of the decade, and my first headlining tour was also her first tour. I have watched Trisha through many phases of her life, and I can tell you that she is in a great place right now. She is balancing her home life with her professional life, her cooking career with her singing career, and indulgence with intelligence. This book reflects exactly where Trisha is in her life. She has found the balance between food that is good and food that is good for you—and she is determined to make meals that are both.

After releasing her first two cookbooks, Trisha noticed a common theme in the questions she would get from people who owned them. Folks were very concerned when it came to the food they were serving and how it affected their family's health. I would overhear women say, "My husband loves your dishes, but he has high cholesterol or high blood pressure." Then they would ask *the* question: "Do you have any suggestions on how to make these dishes healthier without making them taste any different?" I would watch her walk with each woman and take her to different parts of the store and pick out products, read labels, discuss the options . . . it was really cool to witness. It was as if she were on a mission. Much later it finally hit me. The reason Miss Yearwood was on this mission was because she knew it would not be long before she was that woman, and the man she would be worrying about would be me.

So she decided not to wait until we were older, but to start planning for a healthier life now. What has happened in the past five years has been a miracle for me. I have always had problems with high cholesterol and high blood pressure . . . always. But on my last checkup, my doctor came in, put the results down on the desk, and jokingly said, "These results *cannot* be yours." I smiled. I have not had a report like that in my life . . . ever. I know

it is because Trisha has found ways to replace ingredients that create a
more unhealthy experience with ingredients that, I believe, actually fight
and repair the damage caused by my own poor choices—*and* I have yet to
sacrifice taste! Once you find the person you want to spend the rest of your
life with, your only enemies are time and the quality of life during that time.
Miss Yearwood is trying to make our time the best it can be, and I am very
proud to know she is doing the same thing for all of those you and I love.

Garth Brooks
(aka Mr. Yearwood)

introduction

In the five years since *Home Cooking with Trisha Yearwood* came out, a lot has changed in my life. My experiences have definitely altered the way I look at food. I still agree with the famous quote "Everything in moderation, including moderation," but I have adopted an 80/20 rule when it comes to my delicate relationship with food: 80 percent of the time I make good choices; 20 percent of the time I let myself splurge a little. Growing up enjoying my parents' and grandparents' comfort foods taught me early on about taste. It was always hard for me to go on a traditional *diet* because I had been led to believe I had to sacrifice flavor to shed a few pounds, so that effort never lasted very long. This girl likes good food! I am not one of those people who gets so busy with my day that I suddenly think to myself, "Wow, I forgot to eat lunch!" That never happens to me. *Never.* I think about food all the time, so making peace with eating is a daily battle for me. I won't say I've completely figured it out, but I will say that right now, I win that battle more days than I lose it, and I believe that's the key.

In my first two cookbooks, my mom, my sister, and I wrote about our family history—recipes that have been passed down for generations. My life now focuses on finding new recipes that feel like classics and on applying healthy twists to foods that my family already loves. I don't want my family or yours to feel like they're sacrificing flavor in order to eat better. I can't imagine not having great comfort foods like Chicken Tortilla Casserole and Slow

Cooker Georgia Pulled-Pork Barbecue. By the same token, I can't imagine my life now without lighter options that help me maintain my goals, like Tofu Ricotta Lasagna or Chickless Pot Pie, a plant-based veggie pot pie that my mama created for herself while battling breast cancer.

I'm a singer and a cook—not a nutritionist. I read books, blogs, and articles every day, just like you do, about what's healthy and what's not. I wish I had the definitive answer, but I don't. The common denominator in all the information seems to be to eat more fruits and vegetables, eat less sugar, and move more. I love knowing that when I make the dairy-free version of Tomato Bisque with Homemade Croutons for my husband (one of his favorite winter meals!), he's not putting any cholesterol in his body. That helps me sleep better at night! After losing my dad to complications from diabetes and my mom to cancer and turning fifty myself, I had to really take a hard look at what I want my future to look like. I believe that although we can't control everything that happens to our bodies, we have the opportunity to control a lot more than we think, and food is a great place to start.

Trisha's Table is just that—it's what we eat at my house. It's variety and balance. This book marries the past (think Cornbread-Chili Casserole and Glazed Lemon Cookies) with the future (Garth's Taco Pizza and Avocado Pineapple Salsa). I relied heavily on my sister Beth's knowledge of healthy eating, because she's been doing it successfully for more than ten years now. She looks and feels great. She's my role model on so many levels! In this book, I've included only healthier substitutions that I absolutely LOVE. I'll explain exactly what these new ingredients are—there are just a few things you need in order to totally transform a recipe. For instance, when you see how easy it is to make cashew cream, you'll be amazed by the richness it adds to creamy dishes like Tomato Bisque, with zero cholesterol!

Trisha's Table is a bridge between southern classics and the way the New South eats . . . with an occasional slice of chocolate cake thrown in! I hope you find the perfect balance in your own lives and for your families. Be well!

Love,

Trisha

breakfast

Breakfast Burritos

Cinnamon Orange Rolls

Granola Parfaits

Cran-Apple Crisp

Holiday French Toast

Hummingbird Pancakes

Isabelle's Crepes

Mel's Banana Muffins

Spinach Frittata

breakfast burritos

4 large whole wheat tortillas

1 (10-ounce) package fully cooked breakfast sausage links (I like Jimmy Dean's turkey sausage)

2 tablespoons olive oil

6 large eggs (or substitute 6 large egg whites)

¼ cup chives, finely chopped

3 tablespoons whole milk or heavy cream

½ teaspoon salt

¼ teaspoon freshly ground black pepper

2 tablespoons salted butter

4 ounces sharp Cheddar cheese, grated

½ cup Avocado Pineapple Salsa (page 34)

4 lime wedges

Hot sauce, optional

trisha tip

The Avocado Pineapple Salsa recipe makes 2 cups. Serve extra on the side with bagel chips, or store in an airtight container in the refrigerator for up to a week.

I'm always looking for a break from the usual breakfast. I tend to get into a pattern—scrambled eggs, wheat toast with peanut butter, cereal, back to scrambled eggs! These breakfast burritos take just minutes to put together, especially if you make the yummy avocado salsa the night before. Use some in your morning burrito, and save the rest to serve with chips for an afternoon snack. This tasty meal always gets my day going right! **MAKES 4 BURRITOS**

Preheat the oven to 250°F.

Place the tortillas on a baking sheet and heat in the oven until warmed through and softened, about 5 minutes.

Meanwhile, using kitchen shears, cut the sausage links into ¼-inch pieces. Heat the oil in a small skillet over medium-low heat until shimmering, about 2 minutes, then add the sausage and heat, stirring frequently, until warmed through, about 4 minutes. In a medium bowl, whisk the eggs. Add the chives, milk, salt, and pepper.

In a medium nonstick skillet over medium heat, melt the butter, then add the egg mixture, and using a rubber spatula, push the eggs toward the center of the pan until the mixture is no longer runny. Add the cheese and gently toss until cooked to desired consistency.

Divide the eggs evenly among the tortillas. Top with sausage and 2 tablespoons of the prepared Avocado Pineapple Salsa. Squeeze a lime wedge over the salsa, and add a dash of hot sauce, if desired.

Starting from one end, roll the tortilla once, then fold in the sides and continue rolling until fully enclosed.

cinnamon orange rolls

DOUGH

1 package active dry yeast (2¼ teaspoons)

¼ cup + 1 teaspoon granulated sugar

¼ cup hot water

¼ cup olive oil

1 tablespoon freshly grated orange zest

¼ cup freshly squeezed orange juice

½ cup whole milk

3½ cups all-purpose flour

1 teaspoon salt

Vegetable oil, for the bowl

FILLING

3 tablespoons salted butter, softened

1 cup firmly packed light brown sugar

1½ tablespoons ground cinnamon

GLAZE

2 cups confectioners' sugar (see Trisha Tip, page 207)

3 tablespoons freshly squeezed orange juice

Weekends are big breakfast time for us. I have to confess that during the busy week, I usually grab some peanut butter toast and a banana for my morning meal, but weekends are different. They're for sleeping in and waking up to cook for everybody. We make the usual— eggs, biscuits, bacon, you name it—but I like to include something sweet, too. Cinnamon rolls are always a big hit at my house. The addition of orange juice in the dough and in the glaze makes them extra special. **MAKES 12 ROLLS**

In a small bowl, combine the yeast, 1 teaspoon of the sugar, and the hot water, whisking to mix. Set aside for 10 minutes, allowing the yeast to dissolve and fully activate. It should bubble around the edges and almost double in size. Meanwhile, in a medium bowl, whisk together the remaining sugar, oil, orange zest, orange juice, and milk, and set aside.

Using an electric mixer fitted with the paddle attachment, combine the flour and salt. Add the yeast mixture and the orange juice mixture, and beat until the dough forms a ball, 2 to 3 minutes. Switch out the paddle for the dough hook, and knead the dough until fairly smooth, 4 to 5 minutes. If the dough is too sticky, add more flour, one tablespoon at a time.

Lightly coat a large bowl with vegetable oil and add the dough. Cover the bowl with plastic wrap, and then allow the dough to rise until it doubles in size, about 1 hour at room temperature.

recipe continues

Preheat the oven to 350°F and spray a 9 × 13-inch baking dish with cooking spray. Set aside.

On a lightly floured surface, roll the dough into a large rectangle, about ¼ inch thick. Be sure the rectangle is slightly bigger than the pan you're going to bake in. Spread the butter over the dough, leaving a ¼-inch border on all sides. Sprinkle the dough with the brown sugar, then the cinnamon. Starting with one longer edge, roll the dough into a cylinder and pinch the ends together to seal completely. Cut into 12 rolls and place in the prepared baking dish. Cover the dish with plastic wrap and allow the rolls to rise until they double in size, about 30 minutes at room temperature.

After the rolls have doubled in size, remove the plastic wrap and bake uncovered until lightly brown, 25 to 30 minutes.

Meanwhile, in a medium bowl, whisk together the confectioners' sugar and orange juice until smooth. While the rolls are still warm, drizzle them with glaze and serve.

My niece Ashley, helping her granddaddy make biscuits (1995).

granola parfaits

2¼ cups old-fashioned rolled oats (not quick-cooking)

1 cup sweetened shredded coconut

1 cup slivered almonds

¼ cup vegetable oil

¼ cup honey, plus more for drizzling

¾ cup dried cranberries

¾ cup golden raisins

⅓ cup shelled and salted sunflower seeds

2 cups low-fat plain Greek yogurt

Fresh berries, optional

Here's the thing about granola. I never ate it growing up, and even when all my health-conscious friends told me how awesome it was, I was still skeptical. One day, between flights in an airport, I was hungry and looking for a snack. I went through the sundries shop and didn't see anything that looked appetizing except this beautifully swirled granola parfait. My time had come! It was good. Really good. I liked the sweet granola with the tart yogurt. My friend Mel took granola to a whole new level by showing me how to make my own. Life changed! It takes twenty minutes and is easily stored in plastic bags to throw in my purse for take-along snacks. If I'm on the road, all I have to do is buy a tub of Greek yogurt and mix in this yummy homemade granola, and I have my own "road parfait." If you're a granola skeptic as I used to be, welcome to paradise. You're gonna love this!

MAKES 4 PARFAITS

Preheat the oven to 350°F. In a large bowl, toss together the oats, coconut, and ¾ cup of the almonds. In a small bowl, whisk together the oil and honey, then stir into the oats mixture. Spread the mixture in an even layer on a rimmed baking sheet. Bake until golden brown, 17 to 20 minutes, stirring occasionally. Remove from the oven and allow to cool completely, about 20 minutes.

Transfer the mixture to a large bowl and add the cranberries, raisins, and sunflower seeds. Line up parfait, wine, or tall glasses. Carefully spoon a large dollop of the yogurt into each and top with a large spoonful of granola. Add a few berries, if using, then drizzle with honey. Repeat the layers once more in each glass. Top the parfaits with the remaining slivered almonds for garnish.

cran-apple crisp

FILLING

1 tablespoon salted butter, softened

1 (14-ounce) can whole-berry cranberry sauce

¾ cup granulated sugar

2 tablespoons all-purpose flour

5 medium Granny Smith apples, peeled, cored, and sliced into ¼-inch slices

TOPPING

¼ cup chopped pecans

1 cup quick-cooking oats

⅓ cup firmly packed light brown sugar

⅓ cup all-purpose flour

1 teaspoon ground cinnamon

¼ cup (½ stick) salted butter, melted

It's a shame that most folks only think of eating cranberry sauce during the holidays, and even then, some people put it on their plates just to be nice. Can you believe that? I can personally eat an entire bowl of cranberry sauce in one sitting, and it's seriously good spread on turkey sandwiches—not just on Thanksgiving and Christmas. If you're on the cranberry fence, a bowl of this warm, crunchy goodness (maybe even topped with a little vanilla ice cream) will cause you to reevaluate! **SERVES 8 TO 10**

Preheat the oven to 375°F. Coat a 9 × 9-inch baking dish with softened butter. Set aside.

In a large mixing bowl, stir together the cranberry sauce, granulated sugar, and the 2 tablespoons of flour. Add the apples to the cranberry mixture, tossing to coat, and pour the mixture into the prepared baking dish.

To make the crumb topping, in the same mixing bowl, stir together the pecans, oats, brown sugar, ⅓ cup flour, cinnamon, and melted butter. Sprinkle the mixture over the apples in the dish and bake until golden brown, 35 to 40 minutes. Serve warm or at room temperature.

holiday french toast

3 medium ripe bananas

3 tablespoons half and half

2 large eggs

1½ teaspoons ground cinnamon

1 teaspoon pumpkin pie spice

1 teaspoon vanilla extract

6 to 8 thick-cut slices bread of your choice (I like honey wheat)

6 to 8 tablespoons salted butter, for pan frying

Confectioners' sugar, for sprinkling

Maple syrup, for serving

French toast is special-occasion breakfast at my house. The cinnamon and pumpkin pie spice in this recipe make it smell and taste like Christmas to me, so I named it Holiday French Toast. Of course, it doesn't have to be a special holiday to have this awesomeness for breakfast any day of the week—or any time of year! **MAKES 6 TO 8 PIECES**

In a large bowl, mash the bananas, then whisk them together with the half and half, eggs, cinnamon, pumpkin pie spice, and vanilla until fully combined. Pour the mixture onto a large plate with edges, such as a pie plate. Dip the bread slices into the mixture, being sure to coat both sides evenly.

Melt 2 tablespoons of the butter in a medium skillet over medium heat, and pan-fry two slices at a time until golden brown, about 2 minutes per side. Remove from the skillet, add more butter, 2 tablespoons at a time, and the remaining pieces of battered bread, 2 at a time, to the skillet and cook.

Stack on a plate, sprinkle with confectioners' sugar, and serve with maple syrup.

hummingbird pancakes

1½ cups baking mix
(I like Bisquick)

½ teaspoon
ground cinnamon

1½ cups half and half

1 cup mashed bananas
(about 2 large)

½ cup crushed
pineapple, drained

¼ cup sugar

1 large egg

3 tablespoons salted
butter, melted

½ cup pecans,
finely chopped

Sliced bananas and
strawberries,
for serving

Hummingbird cake has been popular in the South since the mid-nineteenth century. It has always included some combination of bananas, pineapple, and pecans, but I have no idea how it got its name. Maybe it has something to do with being drawn to the sweetness the way hummingbirds are drawn to nectar! To be on the safe side, don't eat them outside . . . you might have to share with those tiny birds! These pancakes are so good, you don't even need syrup. Just top them with your favorite fruit, and dig in! **SERVES 4**

Heat a nonstick griddle. In a large bowl, combine the baking mix and the cinnamon. In a separate bowl, whisk together the half and half, bananas, pineapple, sugar, egg, and butter until smooth. Add the wet mixture to the dry, and stir just until the dry ingredients are moistened, taking care not to overmix. Fold in the pecans.

Using a ¼-cup measure, pour the batter onto the griddle and cook for 2 to 4 minutes, watching for the tops of the pancakes to start bubbling. Flip and cook for 2 to 4 more minutes. Repeat the process with the remaining batter. Serve with sliced bananas and strawberries.

trisha tip

If you don't have an electric griddle, use a nonstick skillet over medium heat.

isabelle's crepes

1 cup all-purpose flour

¼ cup sugar

5 large eggs

¼ cup (½ stick) salted butter, melted

½ teaspoon freshly grated lemon zest

2 cups whole milk

Fruit and confectioners' sugar, for serving

trisha tip

If your crepes are falling apart when you flip them, you are turning them too soon. Loosen them from the pan with a spatula and cook for 10 more seconds before flipping.

My friend Lisa sells merchandise on the road for artists, including me, so I call her the T-shirt goddess. She's great with people and always has a smile for everyone—she's one of the hardest-working gals I know! Lisa's true talent is art. She can draw anything, and, as a matter of fact, has designed many of the T-shirts, hats, and sweatshirts that you may have seen of mine over the years on tour. But I think Lisa shines most when she paints. She transforms a canvas into something magical. She loves to travel, and especially loves Europe. On one of her visits to France, she got this recipe for crepes from her friend Isabelle, who got it from her sister Françoise. Imagine you're having these with a nice espresso on the Riviera when you make them! Bon appetit! **SERVES 4**

Lightly grease a crepe pan or a shallow sauté pan with oil or butter. Set aside.

In a medium bowl, whisk together the flour, sugar, eggs, butter, and lemon zest. Slowly add the milk while continuing to whisk. The batter should have the consistency of cream.

Heat the greased pan over medium heat for about 1 minute. Using a ⅓-cup measure, pour the mixture into the pan. Tilt the pan to be sure the batter spreads out evenly over the bottom in a thin layer. Cook for 2 minutes, or until the crepe is light brown on the underside (check using a spatula to gently lift up one edge of the crepe), then flip to cook the other side for 30 seconds more. Repeat with the remaining batter. Serve topped with the fruit of your choice, or as I prefer, just a sprinkle of confectioners' sugar.

mel's banana muffins

1 cup whole wheat flour

¾ cup all-purpose flour

¼ cup wheat germ

1 teaspoon baking soda

½ teaspoon salt

½ cup (1 stick) unsalted butter, softened (see Trisha Tip)

⅓ cup granulated sugar

⅓ cup firmly packed light brown sugar

2 large eggs, at room temperature

¾ cup mashed bananas (about 2 medium)

⅓ cup 2% milk

1 teaspoon vanilla extract

1 cup blueberries

trisha tip

If a recipe calls for unsalted butter and you have only salted butter on hand, cut the amount of salt in the recipe ingredients by half. Salt is a preservative, so remember that salted butter will last for up to 3 months in your fridge, while unsalted butter will last about a month.

My friend Melissa turned me on to these power muffins. The combination of whole wheat flour with all-purpose flour gives you all the benefits of whole wheat, but with a lighter texture. Wheat germ is good stuff because it's the most vitamin- and mineral-rich part of the wheat kernel, but you don't taste it in the muffin—your kids will love these for breakfast and never know you're sneaking in extra nutrients! I love the taste of bananas mixed with blueberries, but I encourage you to try mixing it up by using different fruits. Add a half cup semisweet chocolate chips to this batter for an extra sweet surprise. MAKES 12 MUFFINS

Preheat the oven to 375°F. Line a 12-cup muffin pan with paper liners and set aside.

In a medium bowl, whisk together the flours, wheat germ, baking soda, and salt. Using an electric mixer, beat the butter and sugars together until light and fluffy, about 5 minutes. Add the eggs, one at a time, beating well after each addition.

In a separate bowl, mash the bananas with a fork. Stir in the milk and vanilla. With the mixer on low, alternately add ⅓ of the flour mixture and ½ of the banana mixture to the butter mixture, beginning and ending with the flour mixture. Mix until just combined. Fold in the blueberries.

Divide the batter among the muffin cups. Bake for 20 to 24 minutes, or until a toothpick inserted in the center of a muffin comes out clean.

spinach frittata

4 large eggs

½ cup heavy cream

½ teaspoon salt

¼ teaspoon freshly
ground black pepper

1 cup shredded
Swiss cheese

1 cup lengthwise-halved
grape tomatoes

2 tablespoons
salted butter

1 small onion,
finely chopped

4 cups fresh
baby spinach

trisha tip

**I use my mama's
seasoned cast-iron
skillet for this frittata.**

*I love quiche, but when I'm hungry, I don't want to wait
an hour for the crust to bake. I figured out that if I made
quiche into a frittata, I could ditch the crust altogether and
be eating in just 15 minutes! Even though this is a rich egg
dish, all that spinach gives me the good nutrients I need to
make it through my day. For a complete breakfast, I like
to add a cup of crumbled cooked sausage before baking.*

SERVES 4

Preheat the oven to broil.

In a medium bowl, whisk together the eggs, cream, salt, and
pepper until smooth. Fold in the cheese and tomatoes and set
aside.

In a 9-inch oven-safe frying pan over medium heat, melt
the butter. Add the onion and sauté until softened, about
5 minutes. Add the spinach and cook until just wilted, about
2 minutes. Pour the egg mixture over the spinach, and cook
until almost set, 2 to 4 minutes.

Transfer the pan to the oven and broil until golden brown on
top, 5 to 7 minutes. Remove from the oven and turn out onto a
serving plate.

Edamame Parmesan
(page 44)

snacks & appetizers

Avocado Pineapple Salsa

Pistachio Cheese Dip

Caramelized Onion Dip

Basil Pesto Pizza

Black Pepper Tofu with
Soy Dipping Sauce

Cream Cheese Roll-Ups
(aka Redneck Sushi)

Edamame Parmesan

Potato Skins

Emmett's Dill Pickles

Garth's Taco Pizza

Kale Chips

Lory's Salsa Ranchera

Unfried Pickles

Pickled Okra

Power Balls

Quinoa Burger with
Yogurt Sauce

avocado pineapple salsa

3 medium avocados, diced

¼ cup finely chopped sweet onion (I like Vidalia)

½ cup finely chopped pineapple

⅔ cup quartered grape tomatoes (about 16)

2 tablespoons freshly squeezed lime juice

¼ teaspoon garlic salt

1 teaspoon red pepper flakes

¼ cup finely chopped fresh cilantro (optional)

Freshly ground black pepper to taste

Baked pita chips, for serving

This salsa was inspired by putting all of the things Garth loves into one dip—he makes a killer guacamole complete with a tomato rose garnish. (Really, he does!) For me, the sweet pineapple is what makes this dish special. It's like having your salsa and your guacamole all in one fanstastic bite! **MAKES 2 CUPS**

In a medium bowl, combine the avocado, onion, pineapple, tomatoes, lime juice, garlic, salt, red pepper flakes, and cilantro, if using. Add pepper to taste. Serve with baked pita chips.

pistachio cheese dip

1 cup shelled and chopped raw pistachios

12 ounces cream cheese, softened

16 ounces white Cheddar cheese, grated and at room temperature

½ cup mayonnaise

½ cup whole milk

½ teaspoon garlic salt

½ teaspoon onion powder

½ teaspoon white pepper

½ teaspoon salt

2 teaspoons chopped fresh parsley

1½ teaspoons white vinegar

¼ teaspoon dry dill weed

Crackers or pita chips, for serving

I know it's a pattern with me, but I do love cheese. I try to eat it sparingly these days, but when you combine cheese with pistachios—maybe the best nut on the planet—I can't resist. I indulge in this dip only occasionally and then do a little extra Zumba the next day! **MAKES 2 CUPS**

In a medium microwave-safe bowl, microwave the pistachios on high for 3 minutes to toast them. Allow to cool completely, about 10 minutes.

Using an electric mixer, beat together the cream cheese, Cheddar cheese, mayonnaise, and milk until smooth. Add the garlic salt, onion powder, white pepper, salt, parsley, vinegar, and dill. Fold in the pistachios.

Transfer to a serving bowl, cover with plastic wrap, and refrigerate for 30 minutes to an hour before serving with crackers or pita chips.

trisha tip

Mama taught me how easy it is to toast nuts in the microwave. Just a few minutes, and the flavor really comes through. Her favorite was a raw almond. Cooking time will vary depending on the wattage of your microwave. Mine is 1100 watts. To toast in a conventional oven, preheat to 350°F. Spread the nuts in an even layer on a baking sheet. Roast for 9 to 12 minutes, stirring every 3 minutes, until golden brown. Immediately transfer to a plate to cool.

caramelized onion dip

¼ cup olive oil

3 medium onions, finely chopped

1 teaspoon firmly packed light brown sugar

2 tablespoons balsamic vinegar

½ teaspoon salt

¼ teaspoon freshly ground black pepper

2 garlic cloves, minced

1 cup plain low-fat Greek yogurt

½ cup mayonnaise

½ teaspoon Worcestershire sauce

What did we do before pre-packaged French onion dip came into our lives? I'll tell you what . . . we made our own! Most people don't realize just how easy it is. This particular dip combines mayonnaise with Greek yogurt. Add in caramelized onions, and you've got the perfect homemade dip to spread on your favorite veggies or chips. I'm old school, and like to use Lay's Classic Potato Chips.

MAKES 2 CUPS

In a large saucepan over medium heat, heat the oil until shimmering, about 2 minutes, then add the onions. Cook until the onions start to brown, stirring constantly, about 15 minutes. Stir in the brown sugar, vinegar, salt, and pepper, then reduce the heat to low, and simmer for 20 minutes, stirring occasionally. Add the minced garlic, and continue to cook for another 10 minutes.

Remove the pan from the heat, and allow to cool completely, about 30 minutes. Stir in the yogurt, mayonnaise, and Worcestershire sauce. Store in the refrigerator until ready to serve.

basil pesto pizza

4 tablespoons + 1 cup olive oil

4 medium sweet onions, finely sliced (I like Vidalia)

6 tablespoons whole raw walnuts

4 to 5 garlic cloves, smashed

⅔ cup grated Parmesan cheese

¼ cup freshly squeezed lemon juice (about 1 lemon)

1 teaspoon sea salt, plus a little more for the olive spread

4 cups fresh basil, stems trimmed and roughly chopped

2 cups fresh spinach, loosely packed

1 cup finely chopped Kalamata olives

1 tablespoon balsamic vinegar

3 medium tomatoes, thinly sliced

2 family-size unbaked pizza crusts, white or whole wheat

trisha tip

Using a pastry brush, I brush a tiny amount of olive oil around the pizza crust edges to make them extra brown and crispy!

Once I discovered pesto, I starting looking for more ways to use it in addition to covering my favorite pasta. I was also looking for a way to make a flavorful veggie pizza, so I combined those two ideas. I use this pesto instead of a red sauce, and it's a wonderful substitute. The combination with onions and Kalamata olives makes for a real burst of flavor! MAKES 8 SLICES

Preheat the oven to 425°F.

In a medium saucepan over medium heat, add 2 tablespoons of the olive oil, heat until shimmering, about 2 minutes, then add the onions. Sauté on low until the onions are brown and caramelized, 20 to 30 minutes, stirring occasionally.

Meanwhile, make the pesto. In a food processor, combine the walnuts and 1 cup of the oil and process until smooth, about 1 minute. Add the smashed garlic cloves, Parmesan cheese, lemon juice, and salt and process until blended, about 1 minute. Add 3¾ cups of the chopped basil, reserving ¼ cup for the topping. Add the spinach and process until smooth, about 1 minute.

To make the olive spread, in a medium skillet over medium heat, add the remaining 2 tablespoons of olive oil and heat until shimmering, about 2 minutes. Add the olives and sauté for 5 minutes. Remove from the heat, then add the balsamic vinegar and a little sea salt to taste.

To assemble the pizzas, spread the pizza dough onto two sheet pans or large round pizza pans. Spread the pesto onto the crusts, leaving a ¼-inch border. Top with the caramelized onions, tomatoes, reserved basil, and Kalamata olive mixture. Garnish with a little Parmesan cheese if you like. Bake for 8 to 10 minutes, or until the crusts are golden brown.

black pepper tofu with soy dipping sauce

TOFU

2 (14-ounce) packages firm tofu (I like Nasoya Organic)

¼ cup low-sodium soy sauce

2 tablespoons toasted sesame oil

¾ teaspoon freshly ground black pepper

SAUCE

¼ cup peeled and grated fresh ginger (about a 2-inch piece)

½ cup low-sodium soy sauce

1 teaspoon freshly grated lemon zest

¼ cup + 1 tablespoon freshly squeezed lemon juice

2 teaspoons sesame oil

When it comes to tofu, I've got two words for you: baby steps. Like most of us, I'm a creature of habit in all things, and in food, it's taken me years to open myself up to trying things other than the traditions I grew up on. I've learned one thing: if you don't try it, you'll never know if you like it. Tofu takes on the taste of whatever you cook it in, so the seasoning is the key. This peppered sesame yumminess packs in flavor. The freshness of ginger and lemon mixed with soy sauce and drizzled over creates the burst of flavor we're all looking for. I like to sauté the tofu until it's extra crispy and brown before serving. **SERVES 4**

Cut the tofu crosswise into equal slices, about ¾ inch thick. Cut each piece diagonally into 2 triangles. Drain for 20 minutes according to the Trisha Tip on page 140, then pat dry.

In a 9 × 13-inch baking dish, stir together the ¼ cup of soy sauce, 2 tablespoons oil, and pepper. Add the tofu and turn to coat both sides. In a large skillet over medium heat, sauté the tofu for 4 minutes, then flip and sauté for 2 to 3 more minutes, or until golden on both sides. Transfer to a serving dish.

To make the dipping sauce, in a small bowl, whisk together the ginger, the ½ cup soy sauce, lemon zest, lemon juice, and 2 teaspoons oil. Drizzle over the tofu.

cream cheese roll-ups (aka redneck sushi)

1 pound bacon

2 (8-ounce) packages cream cheese, softened

¼ cup picante sauce (hot)

4 green onions, finely sliced

4 large flour tortillas

16 slices thin deli ham

trisha tip

You can make these roll-ups the night before, chill overnight, and slice and serve the next day.

I tried octopus once, on a dare from one of our daughters, but I'll admit this southern girl isn't much into sushi. Mama always said it was rude to make a face, and instead to just say "No, thank you" if I didn't like something. Uh . . . no, thank you. Those little rolls always looks so cute on the plate, though, so I came up with my own version. I call it redneck sushi. Roll it up, cut it up just like sushi, and snack right alongside your supercool friends who are eating raw octopus. I draw the line at tentacles! **MAKES 4 ROLLS, 8 PIECES EACH**

In a large skillet over medium heat, use kitchen shears to cut the bacon into small pieces, then cook until crisp, drain on a paper towel–lined plate, and set aside.

In a medium mixing bowl, using a hand mixer, combine the cream cheese, picante sauce, and green onions. Divide evenly and spread among the tortillas, leaving a ½-inch border all around. Top each tortilla with 4 slices of ham and bacon pieces. Roll each tortilla into a cylinder, wrap each in plastic wrap, and refrigerate for 1 hour.

Remove the rolls from the fridge and discard the plastic wrap. Cut each roll into 1-inch pieces, discarding the uneven ends (or taste them while preparing, as I do!). If you like, for easy serving, stick toothpicks in the roll 1 inch apart before cutting.

edamame parmesan

1 (12-ounce) package frozen shelled edamame, thawed

2 tablespoons olive oil

¼ cup grated Parmesan cheese

¼ teaspoon garlic powder

Salt and freshly ground black pepper to taste

I have always loved edamame and usually just boil it in the pod, salt it, and eat it. Tossing it in a little olive oil, adding some Parmesan cheese, then baking it gives the dish a new twist and a slight crunch. This recipe works really well with garbanzo beans, too! **MAKES 1½ CUPS**

Preheat the oven to 400°F. In a medium bowl, toss the edamame with the oil to coat. In a separate small bowl, mix together the Parmesan cheese, garlic powder, salt, and pepper. Add the Parmesan mixture to the edamame and toss to coat.

Spread the edamame onto a jelly roll pan in a single layer and bake until the cheese browns a bit, 10 to 15 minutes, turning once halfway through cooking. Store in an airtight container in the refrigerator for up to 2 weeks.

potato skins

3½ pounds (about 12 medium) red potatoes

2 tablespoons olive oil

8 slices bacon

2 tablespoons salted butter, melted

Salt and freshly ground black pepper to taste

2½ cups (about 10 ounces) grated sharp Cheddar cheese

½ cup sour cream

½ cup finely chopped green onions

Every time I make baked potato soup, I have all these amazing skins left over and I just cannot discard them! I'm that person who eats every single bite of my baked potato, skin and all. Plan to make these skins anytime you're using the flesh of potato for soup, potato pancakes, or any other dish. I use red potatoes, but russets work just fine, too!

MAKES 24 POTATO SKINS

Place the oven rack in the center and preheat the oven to 400°F. Wash the potatoes and pierce them all over with a fork. Rub them with the oil and place on a jelly roll pan. Bake until tender, 45 minutes to 1 hour. Remove the potatoes from the oven and halve lengthwise. Set aside to cool for about 15 minutes. Meanwhile, turn on the broiler.

While the broiler is heating, using kitchen shears, cut the bacon into small pieces and cook in a medium skillet over medium heat until crispy, then drain on a paper towel–lined plate and set aside.

When the potatoes are cool enough to handle, scoop out the flesh and save for another use. Brush the insides of the skins with the melted butter and sprinkle with salt and pepper. Place on a baking sheet and under the broiler until the skins begin to crisp, 2 to 3 minutes. Flip the skins over and broil for another 2 to 3 minutes.

Remove the sheet from the oven and fill each skin with the cheese and the bacon crumbles. Put the sheet back under the broiler until the cheese melts, about 5 minutes. Remove and top with a dollop of sour cream and a few pieces of green onions.

trisha tip

Unlike baking potatoes, which I wrap in foil, I bake these unwrapped for a stronger shell, which keeps them firmer and makes scooping the flesh out easier.

emmett's dill pickles

1 (32-ounce) jar whole dill pickles

1 pound sugar

3 garlic cloves

2 tablespoons hot sauce (I like Tabasco)

trisha tip

You might need a spare quart jar just in case the "fixins" don't all fit back into the one they started in!

Emmett was a friend of Garth's and mine for more than twenty-five years. He passed away a couple of years ago. He's one of those guys whose memory makes me smile every time I think of him because he had such a great sense of humor and would do anything in the world for you. Everyone who knew Emmett loved him, and we all miss him so much that we celebrate his birthday every July for a whole week—we call it the Days of Em! He called this recipe his dill pickle "fixins." I make them every year.

MAKES 1 QUART

Drain the pickles, reserving the juice, and save the jar! Slice the pickles into ⅛-inch slices and put them back into the empty jar. In a large bowl, combine the sugar, garlic cloves, and hot sauce. Add the pickle juice in and stir, then add the mixture back to the sliced pickles in the jar. Put the lid on, and refrigerate for 5 days before serving, stirring a couple of times each day.

Emmett and me (2000).

garth's taco pizza

1 (13.8-ounce) can premade pizza crust dough (I like Pillsbury)

1 (16-ounce) can refried beans

½ cup mild picante sauce

¾ cup sliced green or black olives

8 ounces sharp Cheddar cheese, shredded (about 2 cups)

Salt to taste

1 cup finely diced tomato (about 1 large or 30 grape tomatoes)

12 ounces shredded lettuce (about 1 large head)

¼ cup sour cream

trisha tip

Garth likes extra-mild picante. I use medium to hot.

People always ask me, "Does Garth cook?" and I say "Yes!" I'm not sure they believe me, but he's really the "whatever it takes" guy. He is always ready to make supper if I don't have time, or even if I'm just not in the mood to cook. He came up with this awesome idea for making tacos into pizza—his favorite two meals in one! Add crumbled cooked ground beef or shredded chicken with taco seasoning to give it that classic taco flavor! **MAKES 8 SLICES**

Preheat the oven to 425°F. Roll out the pizza dough and fit onto a 15-inch pizza pan or baking sheet. In a medium bowl, mix together the beans and picante sauce until combined. Spread the mixture onto the crust, leaving a ¼-inch border. Scatter the olives over the crust, then top with the cheese. Bake for 20 minutes, or until the crust is lightly browned.

While the crust is baking, lightly salt the tomatoes, then, in a medium bowl, toss them with the lettuce and sour cream. Once the pizza is out of the oven, top it with the cool lettuce mixture.

kale chips

3 tablespoons olive oil

2 tablespoons apple cider vinegar

2 teaspoons sugar

1½ teaspoons salt

1½ teaspoons garlic powder

¼ teaspoon cayenne pepper

1 pound kale, washed, de-stemmed, and chopped into 1-inch pieces

Kale seems to be all the rage, and I have jumped on the bandwagon like everybody else. I like these "chips" because they combine sweet, salt, and spicy. They're the perfect crunchy snack between meals, and they are loaded with nutrients, especially vitamin K. K for kale! **MAKES 2 CUPS**

Preheat the oven to 350°F, first placing the rack in the center of the oven.

In a large bowl, whisk together the oil, vinegar, sugar, salt, garlic powder, and cayenne until blended. Add the kale and toss to coat.

Spread onto a large baking sheet in a single layer. Bake until crispy, 16 to 20 minutes, turning once during cooking.

lory's salsa ranchera

**6 slices bacon,
cut crosswise into
¼-inch pieces**

**4 medium tomatoes,
cut into quarters**

**1 medium onion,
finely diced**

**3 serrano chiles, whole,
stems cut off**

1 garlic clove, minced

½ teaspoon salt

**¼ teaspoon freshly
ground black pepper**

½ teaspoon cumin

Lory is my guitar player Johnny's wife. I've known them both for more than twenty years, and have had the pleasure of sampling their cooking at band Christmas parties and get-togethers over the years. They are both amazing cooks! Lory always brings this homemade salsa, and it's the best thing I've ever tasted. She was kind enough to share her recipe with me. She says you can leave the bacon out altogether if you want to, but why would you? Bacon equals better! **MAKES 2 CUPS**

In a medium saucepan over medium heat, cook the bacon until done (but soft, not crisp). Do not drain. Add the tomatoes, onion, chiles, garlic, salt, pepper, and cumin. Increase the heat to high and bring the mixture to a boil, then reduce the heat to low and simmer, covered, until the tomatoes soften, about 10 minutes.

Remove the pan from the heat and, using a potato masher, mash until all the peppers and tomatoes are in small chunks. Serve hot over your morning eggs (huevos rancheros), tamales, beans (frijoles), or potatoes (papas), or serve cold with tortilla chips.

*Johnny and me
(2013).*

unfried pickles

2 large eggs

⅓ cup all-purpose flour

1 tablespoon Worcestershire sauce

1 teaspoon hot sauce (I like Tabasco)

1 teaspoon garlic powder

1 teaspoon chili powder

Salt and freshly ground black pepper to taste

1 cup panko bread crumbs

½ cup Parmesan cheese

1 (16-ounce) jar dill pickle slices

My favorite barbecue joint in Oklahoma is a place in Owasso called Trail's End. It's owned and run by my friend John Cash. Yes, John Cash—barbecue master, not country music legend! He serves the best fried pickles on the planet. I wanted to come up with a baked version to make them a little less fattening. My peeps love these. I still eat the fried ones when I go up to Trail's End, though!

SERVES 10 TO 12

Spray a rack with cooking spray, place onto a baking sheet, and set aside (I use a cooling rack). Place the oven's rack in the center of the oven and set to broil.

In a medium bowl, whisk together the eggs, flour, Worcestershire sauce, hot sauce, garlic powder, chili powder, salt, and pepper until combined.

In a separate large bowl, mix together the bread crumbs and Parmesan cheese. Dip the pickles into the egg mixture to fully coat, allowing the excess to drip off.

Transfer the dipped and drained pickles to the bowl of crumbs, tossing to coat fully and pressing them to help the crumbs adhere. Lay the coated pickles in an even layer onto the prepared rack. Place in the oven and broil for 4 minutes, then turn the pickles and broil until brown and crispy all over, about another 4 minutes.

trisha tip

If you don't have a cooling rack, you can broil these directly on a baking sheet, but they will not crisp up quite as much.

pickled okra

8 (1-pint) canning jars
with lids and rings

4 cups white vinegar

½ cup pickling salt

¼ cup sugar

4 cups water

2½ pounds small
fresh okra, washed
and drained

8 whole green
chile peppers

8 garlic cloves, sliced

8 teaspoons dill seeds
or 8 fresh springs

trisha tip

Use only whole okra
pods. I learned the hard
way that if you cut the
tips of the pods off to
fit the canning jar, they
become inedible pieces of
salty, vinegary mush!

If you are southern, it is a law that you must know how to can something. We had a big garden when Beth and I were young girls, and Mama canned everything from green beans to tomatoes to cucumbers to creamed corn—you name it. If we grew it and it could be canned, we canned it! It was an all-day process, but come winter, we were glad we'd put in the work to enjoy those fresh vegetables. I think canning is a bit of a lost art that seems to be starting to find its way back into our culture, with more and more folks growing their own food again. That's a good thing! Garth loves pickled okra, and we got a big bagful from our friend John last summer, so I did what all good southern girls do ... I canned them! **MAKES 8 PINTS**

Place the jars, lids, and rings into a large stockpot and cover with water. Set the heat to high, bring to a boil, then reduce the heat to medium-low, and simmer for 5 minutes. Remove the hot jars one at a time from the water using a jar lifter or large tongs. Remove the lids and rings and set aside. Keep the water simmering on the stove for sealing the jars later.

Meanwhile, in a large saucepan over medium-high heat, bring the vinegar, salt, sugar, and water to a boil, then turn off the heat. Pack the whole fresh okra pods, vertically, into each jar until full. Put 1 green chile, 1 garlic clove, and 1 teaspoon (or 1 sprig) of dill into each jar. Pour the vinegar mixture over the okra, dividing evenly among the jars and leaving a ½-inch space at the top. Wipe the rims, then cover immediately with the metal lids, and screw on the rings.

To seal the jars, place them into a canning rack and back into the simmering stockpot of water. Add additional boiling water as needed to cover by 1 to 2 inches. Bring the water to

trisha tip

Pickling salt is sometimes called "canning salt" and is easy to find at your local grocery store. It is regular table salt without the anticaking or iodine additives.

a rolling boil for 10 minutes, then remove from the heat. Cool the jars in the canner water for 5 minutes, then move them to a heatproof surface and continue cooling for 12 to 24 hours.

Test the seals by pressing the center of each lid. If the lid doesn't pop, the jars are properly sealed. If the jar doesn't seal, open it and reprocess with a different jar and lid, or store in the refrigerator to eat within a week. Store sealed jars at room temperature in a cool, dry environment for up to one year.

power balls

2 cups old-fashioned oats

1 cup extra-crunchy peanut butter

½ cup raw honey

½ cup dried cranberries

½ cup mini chocolate chips

½ cup roasted, salted sunflower seeds

2 tablespoons wheat germ

My friend Jan shared her recipe for these protein-packed, no-bake snacks. I keep them in the fridge and will pack a few in a plastic bag to keep in my purse, so if I get stuck out running errands, I don't have the temptation to head for the drive-through. They tide me over and provide good fats. The sweetness of the honey and those little chocolate chips make me feel like I'm treating myself for making a good food choice! **MAKES 30 BALLS**

In a food processor, pulse the oats, peanut butter, honey, cranberries, chocolate chips, sunflower seeds, and wheat germ until fully combined. Cover with plastic wrap and refrigerate for 30 minutes.

Using your hands, form balls (about 1½ tablespoons each) and place on a baking sheet lined with waxed paper. Chill in the refrigerator for 1 hour. Store in an airtight container in the refrigerator for up to 2 weeks.

trisha tip

Use organic wheat germ and raw honey from where you live if possible. It's so good for you!

Beth and me at our first 5K (2013).

quinoa burger with yogurt sauce

BURGERS

⅔ cup red or golden quinoa

2 cups vegetable stock

5 slices wheat bread, crusts cut off and torn

2 large eggs

1 cup grated zucchini (use large holes on the grater)

½ cup grated Parmesan cheese

¼ cup finely chopped chives

2 small garlic cloves, grated

½ teaspoon salt

¼ teaspoon freshly ground black pepper

Olive oil, for pan frying

SAUCE

1 cup plain low-fat Greek yogurt

½ teaspoon Sriracha or hot sauce

1 teaspoon freshly grated lemon zest

1 teaspoon freshly squeezed lemon juice

2 teaspoons chopped fresh chives

Multigrain buns, for serving (optional)

One of the hardest things about changing the way I eat is finding tasty alternatives to my favorite fattier entrées. In an effort to eat more vegetables and to incorporate healthy grains into some of my dishes, I took the concept of a burger and substituted in good-for-you ingredients like zucchini and quinoa. This burger is really like a big, crispy fritter, and the yogurt sauce gives it a real kick. Does this quinoa "burger" take the place of my favorite homemade cheeseburger? Of course not! But it's a healthier alternative that tastes great, and when I do indulge in that real *burger, I enjoy every bite, guilt-free! Truth be told, I find myself craving this crispy burger more and more often.* **MAKES 6 BURGERS**

In a medium saucepan over medium heat, cover the quinoa with the stock and cook until just tender, about 10 minutes. Drain, spread in an even layer on a baking sheet, and allow to cool completely, about 15 minutes.

Meanwhile, in a food processor, pulse the bread until coarse crumbs form. You should have about 1 cup. In a medium bowl, whisk the eggs. Squeeze out and discard all liquid from the zucchini, then add to the eggs. Stir in the Parmesan cheese, chives, garlic, salt, and pepper. Add the cooled quinoa and bread crumbs and gently mix. Cover with plastic wrap and refrigerate for 1 hour.

In a large nonstick sauté pan, heat ¼ inch oil on medium heat until shimmering, about 1 minute. Using your hands, scoop the quinoa mixture and form into six 3-inch balls, flatten slightly into patties, then add to the pan. Heat until

trisha tip

Sriracha, a hot sauce that originates from Thailand, has become all the rage. If you prefer, you can use your favorite hot sauce instead. Mine is Tabasco.

the burger starts to brown on the bottom, 5 to 6 minutes. Flip and continue cooking until browned all over, about 3 more minutes.

To make the yogurt sauce, in a small bowl, mix together the yogurt, Sriracha, lemon zest, lemon juice, and chives until combined. Serve the burgers on multigrain buns slathered with yogurt sauce or on a platter alongside the sauce for dipping.

Creamy Asparagus
Soup (page 65)

soups & salads

Black Bean Chili and Rice

Creamy Asparagus Soup

Tortellini Soup

Kale Soup

Slow Cooker Irish Stout Beef Stew

Vegetable Soup

Wild Rice and Mushroom Soup

Tomato Bisque with Homemade Croutons

Cold Cucumber Salad

Mama's Egg Salad

Billie's Houdini Chicken Salad

Orzo Salad

Chickpea Salad

Roasted Beet Salad with Goat Cheese Croutons

black bean chili and rice

1 tablespoon olive oil

1 large onion, finely chopped

1 green bell pepper, finely chopped

2 garlic cloves, minced

2 (15-ounce) cans black beans, drained and rinsed

1 (14.5-ounce) can fire-roasted diced tomatoes

2 teaspoons chopped fresh oregano or 1 teaspoon dried

1 tablespoon chili powder

Salt and freshly ground black pepper to taste

3 cups cooked rice of your choice

This tasty dish is an easy alternative to traditional meat-based chili. If you're watching your cholesterol, this one's for you! Black beans give you all the protein you need, so you'll be filled up and happy. You'll never miss what's missing, ya know? **SERVES 4 TO 6**

In a large saucepan set over medium heat, heat the olive oil until shimmering, about 30 seconds. Add the onion, bell pepper, and garlic, and sauté until soft and translucent, about 5 minutes. Add the black beans, tomatoes, oregano, and chili powder, and mix to incorporate.

Simmer for 10 to 15 minutes. Add salt and pepper to taste and serve over your favorite rice.

trisha tip

If tomatoes are in season, peel and dice 4 to 5 fresh tomatoes to substitute for the canned tomatoes.

creamy asparagus soup

3 tablespoons olive oil

1 large bunch asparagus, ends trimmed, cut into 2-inch pieces

2 stalks celery, chopped

1 large onion, chopped

8 cups vegetable stock

1 bay leaf

1 cup Cashew Cream (recipe follows) or heavy cream

Salt and freshly ground black pepper

2 cups fresh baby spinach

My friend Tal can make any vegetable taste heavenly— he shared this creamy asparagus soup recipe with me a few years ago. Tal is a vegan chef, and I can tell you from eating this rich soup a lot, you would never know it was vegan. If you're not lactose intolerant or just don't want to venture into the making of cashew cream (though I highly recommend you try it, because it's fun and easy!), you can certainly use regular cream. **SERVES 6**

In a large stockpot over medium heat, heat the olive oil until shimmering, about 1 minute. Add the asparagus, celery, and onion, and sauté until tender, about 10 minutes. Add the vegetable stock and bay leaf, increase the heat to high, and bring to a boil. Then reduce the heat to medium-low and simmer for 30 minutes.

Add the cashew cream and simmer for 10 more minutes. Remove and discard the bay leaf. Season with salt and pepper to taste.

Working in batches, pour the soup into a blender or food processor (I like to use my Vitamix), and blend on high. Add the spinach to the last batch and continue blending until smooth. Pour the soup into a large serving bowl and stir well.

recipe continues

CASHEW CREAM

MAKES 2¼ CUPS

2 cups whole raw cashews

Put the cashews in a bowl and add cold water to cover them. Cover with a lid or plastic wrap and refrigerate overnight. The next day, drain the cashews and rinse under cold water. Put them in a blender with enough fresh cold water to just cover them. Blend on high for several minutes until smooth. Strain the cream through a fine mesh sieve to remove any remaining bits of cashew. (If you are using a high-power blender like a Vitamix, you won't need to strain the cream.) Store refrigerated for 2 weeks or in the freezer for up to 3 months.

tortellini soup

2 tablespoons olive oil

1 medium onion, chopped

1 teaspoon minced garlic

4 carrots, peeled and sliced into ¼-inch coins

8 cups chicken stock

1 cup frozen green peas

1 (12-ounce) container tricolor cheese tortellini

1 (15-ounce) can sweet whole kernel corn, drained

2 cups fresh baby spinach, torn into smaller pieces

Grated Parmesan cheese, for garnish

Minimum prep required—that's music to my ears when I'm in the mood for a quick warm soup on a cool fall night. This one can be in the pot and ready to eat in the time it takes to make a salad to go with it! It's full of delicious vegetables. My husband, affectionately called Gartha Stewart at home, always says, "When in doubt, add tortellini!" I don't think even he could come up with anything to make this soup better! **SERVES 6**

In a large stockpot over medium heat, heat the oil until shimmering, about 2 minutes, then add the onion, garlic, and carrots, and sauté for 5 minutes or until the vegetables are slightly soft. Pour in the chicken stock, increase the heat to high, and bring to a boil. Add the peas, tortellini, and corn and cook for 12 minutes, or according to the package directions for the tortellini.

Remove the stockpot from the heat and add the spinach, stirring until it wilts. To serve, spoon the soup into bowls and top with grated Parmesan cheese.

trisha tip

If fresh corn is in season, substitute kernels from 2 fresh cobs for the canned corn.

kale soup

2 tablespoons olive oil

1 pound pork chorizo, broken into ½-inch pieces

8 cups chicken stock

2 cups Yukon Gold potatoes, cubed

1 large onion, finely chopped

4 garlic cloves, minced

1 pound kale, de-stemmed and chopped into 1-inch pieces

½ cup grated Parmesan cheese

Salt and freshly ground black pepper

A good soup fills you up, warms your tummy, and leaves you nice and satisfied, not overfull. That's exactly what I like about kale soup. Add the fact that kale is one of the most nutritious greens you can possibly eat, and you're all set! You can omit the sausage in this recipe for a "lighter" version, or you can substitute your favorite sausage for the chorizo. SERVES 6

In a large stockpot over medium heat, heat the oil until shimmering, about 2 minutes. Add the chorizo and heat through, 5 to 7 minutes. Add the stock, potatoes, onion, and garlic.

Simmer for 20 to 25 minutes, or until the potatoes are fork tender. Reduce the heat to low, add the kale, and cover. Cook until the kale wilts, 7 to 10 minutes.

Uncover, add the Parmesan cheese, and heat through for about 5 more minutes. Season with salt and pepper to taste.

trisha tip

Chorizo is a spicy pork sausage. Spanish chorizo can be expensive. Mexican chorizo costs less and is a perfectly acceptable substitute. It's usually already cooked and cured when you buy it, so it just needs to be warmed through before eating.

slow cooker irish stout beef stew

¼ cup olive oil

2 medium onions, finely chopped

2 tablespoons tomato paste

2 garlic cloves, minced

3 cups chicken stock

1¼ cups Irish stout beer (I like Guinness Draught)

2 tablespoons firmly packed light brown sugar

2 pounds Yukon Gold potatoes, unpeeled, cut into 1-inch pieces

1 pound carrots, peeled and cut into 1-inch pieces

2 tablespoons finely chopped fresh parsley

½ cup all-purpose flour

½ teaspoon salt

¼ teaspoon freshly ground black pepper

1 (4-pound) boneless beef chuck roast, trimmed and cut into 1½-inch pieces

2 tablespoons salted butter

On those days when winter chills you to the bone, nothing will warm you up quite like a hearty bowl of beef stew. You get all the comfort of "meat and potatoes," and the magic ingredient, Guinness Draught stout, creates the richest-tasting stew you've ever spooned up. After eating this meal, you won't even mind the cold! To make it even thicker, prepare a roux of 4 tablespoons each of salted butter and all-purpose flour in a sauté pan. Cook for 2 minutes, then stir in 2 cups of the stew liquid. Add the mixture to the finished stew. **SERVES 6**

In a large slow cooker, combine the oil, onions, tomato paste, garlic, chicken stock, beer, brown sugar, potatoes, carrots, and parsley. In a separate bowl, mix together the flour, salt, and pepper. Dredge the beef in the flour mixture, shaking off any excess.

In a medium skillet over medium heat, melt the butter, then add the beef and sear until brown, about 1 minute per side. Add the beef to the slow cooker. Cover, and cook on high for 6 hours.

Me and my snowman (1973).

trisha tip

To correct an oversalted soup or stew, add a couple of peeled and quartered white potatoes and cook. They will absorb some of the extra salt.

vegetable soup

¼ cup olive oil

1 pound carrots, peeled and cut into ½-inch pieces

1½ pounds (about 3 medium) onions, finely chopped

2 garlic cloves, minced

2 (28-ounce) cans diced tomatoes, with their juices

1 pound (about ½ small head) green cabbage, shredded

1 (15-ounce) can green beans

12 cups vegetable or chicken stock

2 teaspoons salt

½ teaspoon freshly ground black pepper

1 pound baby spinach

This recipe is the Trisha version of that low-calorie, low-fat cabbage soup everybody makes when they're on a diet. What makes it different? You just leave out all the vegetables you don't like! It is a great soup when you're counting calories, but I love cabbage so much, especially in a winter soup. In fact, I usually double the cabbage that this recipe calls for. Add cooked macaroni noodles to this soup and call it dinner! **SERVES 6**

In a large stockpot over medium heat, heat the oil until shimmering, about 2 minutes. Add the carrots, onions, and garlic, and sauté until they begin to soften, about 12 minutes, stirring occasionally. Add the tomatoes, cabbage, beans, stock, salt, and pepper.

Increase the heat to medium-high, and bring to a boil, stirring occasionally, then reduce the heat to low, cover, and simmer for 10 minutes. Add the spinach, cover, and continue to simmer until it wilts, about 5 minutes more. Freeze leftovers in 2-cup portions and enjoy all winter.

trisha tip

I use canned Blue Lake green beans in this soup. They are a bush-type snap bean that was developed from the Blue Lake pole bean. I like them because they aren't stringy like some beans can be. If you like the al dente feel of green beans, use fresh ones—ends trimmed, and cut into thirds.

wild rice and mushroom soup

3 tablespoons olive oil

1 tablespoon salted butter

1 cup finely chopped onion (about 1 medium)

¾ cup carrots (about 3 medium), peeled and finely chopped

2 garlic cloves, minced

2 cups (about 12 ounces) fresh cremini mushrooms, quartered

6 cups chicken stock, plus more as needed

1 cup wild rice

2 cups cooked diced chicken breast (optional)

Salt and freshly ground black pepper

Beth really had the whole "healthier eating" thing down way before I did. She's been eating wild rice for years and telling me the benefits of using it in recipes over standard white rice. Wild rice is low in calories, fat, and sugar and is full of important nutrients, including vitamins B, D, and E. It's also high in fiber and protein and doesn't contain any cholesterol, sodium, or gluten. I finally get it! This soup made me a believer. Add chicken and this dish makes a great weekend lunch or weeknight supper. Oh, and thanks, Beth—you were right. You have that in writing now. You're welcome! **SERVES 6**

In a large saucepan over medium heat, heat the oil and butter until the oil is shimmering and the butter is melted, about 2 minutes. Add the onion and carrots and sauté until the onions are tender, 5 to 8 minutes. Add the garlic and mushrooms and cook for 5 minutes more.

Add the stock and wild rice. Bring the mixture to a boil, then reduce the heat to low, cover, and simmer until the wild rice is tender, about 20 minutes. If using, add in the diced chicken and stir to combine. Season with salt and pepper to taste.

trisha tip

Some of the stock will be absorbed into the rice as it cooks. Add more stock and heat through before serving if necessary.

tomato bisque with homemade croutons

¼ cup (½ stick) salted butter

1 medium onion, chopped

1 medium carrot, peeled and chopped

1 stalk celery, chopped

3 garlic cloves, smashed

2 tablespoons all-purpose flour

5 cups vegetable stock

1 (28-ounce) can whole fire-roasted tomatoes, with their juices

1 tablespoon minced fresh parsley

1 teaspoon freshly picked whole thyme leaves

1 bay leaf

Salt and freshly ground black pepper

1½ cups Cashew Cream (page 66) or heavy cream

Homemade Croutons (recipe follows)

This soup is the most impressive in my arsenal. It tastes so rich and creamy, you'd swear you were at a gourmet restaurant instead of sitting at my dinner table! Homemade croutons make it extra good. I cook it up for my family all winter long, and they can't get enough! **SERVES 6**

Place a large stockpot over medium heat. Add the butter and stir until melted. Add the onion, carrot, celery, and garlic, and cook for 10 minutes, stirring frequently. Sprinkle the flour over the vegetables and continue cooking and stirring until the flour browns slightly, about 2 minutes.

Add the stock, tomatoes with their juices, parsley, thyme, and bay leaf. Increase the heat to high, and bring to a boil. Then reduce the heat to medium-low and simmer for 30 minutes. Season with salt and pepper to taste. Stir in the cream and continue to simmer for 10 minutes, taking care not to let the soup boil. Remove and discard the bay leaf. Working in batches, pour the soup into a blender or food processor, and blend on high for several minutes, until very smooth. Ladle into bowls and garnish with croutons.

trisha tip

Make this soup dairy-free: Substitute Earth Balance Original for the butter in the soup and nutritional yeast for the Parmesan cheese in the croutons. Nutritional yeast has a strong nutty, cheesy flavor. It contains vitamin B12 and is usually found in the bulk aisle of most natural food stores. It's great sprinkled on popcorn or pasta, too!

HOMEMADE CROUTONS

MAKES 4 CUPS

1 day-old baguette, cubed

¼ cup olive oil

¼ cup grated Parmesan cheese

2 teaspoons garlic powder

1 teaspoon salt

½ teaspoon freshly ground black pepper

Preheat the oven to 400°F. Put the cubed bread in a large bowl and set aside. In a medium bowl, whisk together the oil, Parmesan cheese, garlic powder, salt, and pepper. Pour the oil mixture over the cubed bread, tossing to coat. Arrange in an even layer on a baking sheet and bake for 10 to 15 minutes or until golden brown. Add to soups or salads. Store in an airtight container for up to 2 weeks.

cold cucumber salad

1 teaspoon salt

1 cup white vinegar

1½ cups sugar

1 teaspoon celery seed

¼ cup vegetable oil

5 cups cucumber slices
(see Trisha Tip)

1 medium sweet onion,
thinly sliced in rings

1 large red or yellow bell
pepper, thinly sliced

Like many southern gardeners, we usually have tons *of cucumbers each summer, and anyone who comes over can't leave without a to-go bag! Here's a cool summer salad that combines sweet and savory—and it will keep in the fridge for days. With this dish in your repertoire, you* won't *find yourself begging your friends to take cucumbers off your hands!* **SERVES 4 TO 6**

In a medium saucepan over high heat, bring the salt, vinegar, sugar, celery seed, and oil to a boil, then remove the pan from the heat and allow to cool, about 20 minutes. In a large bowl, toss the sliced cucumbers, onion, and bell pepper with the liquid mixture and refrigerate overnight. Serve cold.

trisha tip

Before slicing the cucumbers, score the skins all over vertically with a fork, but do not peel them. Doing so allows the liquid to better penetrate the skins. Try Kirby cucumbers if you can find them. They are smaller than regular cucumbers and are very crunchy and mild in flavor. Perfect for salads!

mama's egg salad

1 dozen large eggs

½ cup mayonnaise
(I like Hellmann's)

2 tablespoons
yellow mustard

2 tablespoons
chopped chives

Salt and freshly ground
black pepper to taste

My mama always managed to get supper on the table, no matter what was going on. She had a full-time job, raised two daughters, made prom dresses, permed hair—you name it! She was a superwoman and a wonderful role model for Beth and me. Egg salad was one of those classic mom things that she could always put together, because we always had eggs in the fridge. I think that's why the recipe is so simple. Simple is best! I just added the chives to her recipe. Look at me, being all fancy! **MAKES 4 CUPS**

In a large stockpot set over high heat, cover the eggs with water and bring to a boil. Turn off the heat, cover, and let sit for 20 minutes. Pour the hot water off the eggs, replace with cold water, and allow to sit for 5 minutes more. Crack and peel the eggs and store refrigerated in a plastic bag until cold, at least 3 hours or overnight.

In a large bowl, using an egg slicer or a knife, finely chop the boiled eggs. Add the mayonnaise, mustard, chives, salt, and pepper, and mix until blended. Spread on your favorite bread, or enjoy on a large lettuce leaf like my mama used to do!

billie's houdini chicken salad

4 boneless, skinless chicken breasts

½ cup low-fat plain Greek yogurt

½ cup seedless Concord grapes, halved

½ cup slivered almonds

½ cup finely chopped pecans

¼ cup dried cranberries

2 small Granny Smith apples, finely diced

½ small red onion, finely chopped

Salt and freshly ground black pepper

Toasted bread or crackers, for serving

Billie Jo Flanagan is a friend of mine. She's also my personal trainer—and a two-time national championship gymnast! She created this amazing salad using the creaminess of Greek yogurt. My mama named it Houdini salad because it magically escapes the high calories of a traditional Waldorf salad while tasting just as delicious!

SERVES 4

In a large stockpot over high heat, cover the chicken with water and bring to a boil. Cook for 20 minutes, or until tender. Drain and set aside to cool completely, about 20 minutes, then shred or dice.

In a large bowl, mix together the chicken, yogurt, grapes, almonds, pecans, cranberries, apples, and onion. Season with salt and pepper to taste. Serve on toasted bread or with crackers.

orzo salad

4 cups chicken stock

1½ cups dry orzo

1 (15-ounce) can chickpeas (garbanzo beans), drained and rinsed

1½ cups (about 25) grape tomatoes, halved

1 small red onion, finely chopped

½ cup feta cheese, crumbled

½ cup pitted and halved Kalamata olives

3 tablespoons red wine vinegar

3 tablespoons olive oil

Salt and freshly ground black pepper to taste

I didn't really know how many of my friends were great cooks until I started writing cookbooks. After that, it seemed to me that everybody had that one recipe, that go-to thing that they make. My friend Shari gave me this orzo salad, and I made it my own by adding olives and feta cheese. Truthfully, I'm always looking to add olives and cheese to any recipe that I think they could enhance! I haven't cooked much with orzo, which is a small-grain pasta that looks like big pieces of rice, but I love the texture of it in this dish. Orzo is Italian, feta is Greek, and I'm southern . . . there's gotta be a good punchline in there somewhere! **SERVES 4**

In a large saucepan over medium heat, add the stock, cover, and bring to a boil. Then add the orzo and cook, stirring frequently, until al dente, 7 to 8 minutes. Drain the orzo in a colander and allow to cool completely.

In a large bowl, toss the orzo, chickpeas, tomatoes, onion, feta, olives, vinegar, oil, salt, and pepper. Serve at room temperature.

chickpea salad

2 (15-ounce) cans chickpeas (garbanzo beans), drained and rinsed

1 large ripe avocado, peeled and pitted

¼ cup finely chopped green onion

¼ cup freshly squeezed lime juice (about 2 limes)

2 tablespoons mayonnaise

2 tablespoons spicy yellow mustard

2 teaspoons minced garlic

Salt and freshly ground black pepper to taste

¼ teaspoon cayenne pepper (optional)

Chickpeas are high in fiber and protein, so they're the perfect snack. I like the taste of them because they remind me a little bit of black-eyed peas, which I love! Combine them with avocado, a little mayo, and a dash of lime juice, and you've got a light-tasting summer salad that will really fill you up. Spread it on toasted multigrain bread and top with fresh cucumber slices and bean sprouts. Yum! SERVES 4

In a medium bowl, using a fork or pastry blender, mash the chickpeas and avocado together until incorporated, but still chunky. Add the green onion, lime juice, mayonnaise, mustard, garlic, salt, and pepper, and stir until mixed. If you want a spicy hot kick, add the cayenne. Refrigerate for at least ½ hour before serving.

trisha tip

You can pulse these ingredients in a food processor for a smoother consistency, but I like the chunkiness of mixing by hand.

roasted beet salad with goat cheese croutons

SALAD
1¼ pounds raw beets, stems trimmed

3 tablespoons olive oil

6 to 8 cups mixed greens

1 Granny Smith apple, cored and sliced into ¼-inch slices

1 cup chopped pecans, toasted

VINAIGRETTE
1 small shallot, finely chopped

½ cup olive oil

¼ cup champagne vinegar

3 tablespoons freshly squeezed orange juice

1 teaspoon honey

1 teaspoon country Dijon mustard (see Trisha Tip, page 97)

Salt and freshly ground black pepper to taste

CROUTONS
¾ cup vegetable oil

8 ounces goat cheese

¼ cup all-purpose flour

1 large egg, beaten

¾ cup panko bread crumbs

1 teaspoon finely chopped fresh parsley

Thanks to my mama, I grew up loving beets. I always laughed when I would hear kids complaining about having to eat them, because we loved them at my house! Mama would chop up pickled beets for salads or just serve them roasted. The beet is an underappreciated vegetable, so I wanted to create a salad that lets it shine! Roasting beets brings out their sweetness, and topping this salad with a citrusy vinaigrette and crunchy pan-fried goat cheese croutons simply takes it over the top! SERVES 4

Preheat the oven to 475°F. Place the beets on aluminum foil and drizzle with the olive oil. Wrap the aluminum foil around them to form a packet and place on a baking sheet. Transfer to the oven and roast until tender, about 1 hour. Remove from the oven and allow the beets to cool slightly in the foil packet, about 5 minutes. Using a paper towel, rub off the skins from the beets. Cut the beets into a total of eight wedges and set aside. Add the beets to a large bowl, along with the mixed greens, apple, and pecans.

To make the vinaigrette, in a medium bowl, whisk together the shallot, olive oil, vinegar, orange juice, honey, mustard, salt, and pepper. Drizzle the prepared salad with the vinaigrette and gently toss to combine. Set aside.

To make the croutons, in a medium skillet, heat the oil over medium-high heat until shimmering, about 2 minutes.

Meanwhile, slice the goat cheese into 8 equal rounds. Put the flour, egg, and bread crumbs into three separate shallow dishes. Mix the parsley into the bread crumbs. Coat each cheese round in flour, then egg, then bread crumbs, and place into the skillet. Pan-fry until golden, about 1 minute per side. Transfer to a paper towel–lined rack or plate. Serve the salad on salad plates and top with the croutons.

beef & pork

Beef Stir-Fry

Beef Stroganoff

Beef Brisket

Cornbread-Chili Casserole

Karri's Honey-Marinated Steak

Slow Cooker Georgia Pulled-Pork Barbecue

Pork Tenderloin with Honey Mustard Glaze

Pork, Apricot, and Rosemary Kebabs

Sausage and Peppers

beef stir-fry

1½ pounds skirt steak cut into 4-inch-long pieces, then cut against the grain into ¼-inch-thick slices

Salt and freshly ground black pepper

¼ cup low-sodium soy sauce

1 fresh serrano chile, seeded and finely chopped

2 teaspoons sugar

¼ cup freshly squeezed lime juice (about 3 limes)

2 tablespoons olive oil

2 garlic cloves, grated

1 bunch green onions, thinly sliced

6 ounces fresh mushrooms, sliced

¼ pound snow peas or green beans

1 (12-ounce) can baby corn

Everybody has his or her own version of stir-fry. I like mine with skirt steak because it's inexpensive and cooks quickly. It's perfect for this spicy dish. The best thing about stir-fry is that you can substitute the vegetables you like best. Don't be intimidated by the serrano chile. It is a hot one, but if you seed it, you'll take away some of the fire and still have the perfect spice for this satisfying stir-fry!

SERVES 4

Season the beef with salt and pepper. In a medium bowl, whisk together the soy sauce, chile, sugar, and lime juice until the sugar is dissolved. Add the beef, toss to coat, and set aside.

In a large skillet over medium-high heat, heat the oil until shimmering, about 1 minute. Then add the beef and cook, stirring until cooked through, 3 to 5 minutes.

Remove the beef from the skillet and set aside. Allow the liquid in the pan to reduce until thickened, about 4 minutes. Add the garlic and green onions and cook for 1 minute more. Add the mushrooms, and cook for 2 to 3 minutes more. Add the snow peas and baby corn, and continue cooking until all the vegetables are tender-crisp, about 3 minutes. Return the beef to the skillet and toss to combine.

trisha tip

If you can't find baby corn, use sweet corn niblets or freshly chopped asparagus.

beef stroganoff

2 tablespoons
salted butter

1 small onion,
thinly sliced

1 pound sirloin steak,
sliced in ¼-inch strips

¾ cup beef stock

1 tablespoon ketchup

2 teaspoons minced
garlic (about 3 cloves)

1 tablespoon
all-purpose flour

8 ounces fresh
mushrooms,
thinly sliced

½ cup sour cream

Salt and freshly ground
black pepper to taste

Cooked rice or egg
noodles, for serving

Because the word Stroganoff *sounds a little fancy, this has been Beth's family's go-to special-occasion meal for years. She breaks out her wedding china and serves this dish (usually to the whole family!) on Valentine's Day or on her wedding anniversary. John and Beth have been married for almost thirty years now, so they must be doing something right!* **SERVES 4**

In a large skillet over medium-high heat, melt the butter, about 2 minutes. Add the onion and brown until tender, about 5 minutes, then transfer to a bowl and set aside.

In the same skillet, sauté the steak, then add ½ cup of the stock, the ketchup, and the minced garlic. Cover, reduce the heat to low, and allow the steak to simmer for 20 minutes.

Whisk the flour into the remaining ¼ cup of stock, then add it to the skillet along with the mushrooms. Increase the heat to high, bring to a boil, and boil for 1 minute, stirring constantly. Remove the skillet from the heat and add the sour cream and the reserved onion. Season to taste with salt and pepper. Serve over rice or egg noodles.

trisha tip

To make the steak easier to slice into strips, put it in the freezer for 20 to 30 minutes—just long enough to make it firm, but not frozen.

*Beth and John
on their wedding day
(August 31, 1985).*

beef brisket

1 teaspoon onion salt

1 teaspoon garlic salt

1 teaspoon celery salt

½ bottle (2 ounces) liquid smoke

1 (6-ounce) can tomato paste

3 pounds beef brisket, trimmed

2 large onions, sliced

2 tablespoons olive oil

trisha tip

Keep the brisket warm by placing it in a slow cooker on the warm setting until ready to serve.

My friend Shirley Anne makes this amazing beef brisket and always brings it over on Super Bowl Sunday—or sometimes just on a rainy day, because she's my friend. She and I have shared recipes for years, and I appreciate that she let me have this one. I think this brisket is best made early in the morning, since it has to cook for several hours, and I don't want to wait all day to eat it. Serve it as a sandwich, but eat it on a plate with a fork because you are going to want all that awesome au jus, and it will fall apart on you if you're not careful! **SERVES 6 TO 8**

In a small bowl, combine the onion salt, garlic salt, and celery salt. In a separate bowl, combine the liquid smoke and the tomato paste. Rub the tomato mixture over the entire brisket and sprinkle both sides with the salt mixture. Transfer to aluminum foil, wrap, and refrigerate overnight.

Remove the brisket from the fridge the next day and allow to come to room temperature, about 1 hour.

Preheat the oven to 375°F. Place the sliced onions in the bottom of a large roasting pan or stockpot, and toss with the olive oil to coat. Arrange in an even layer, and put the brisket on top. Cover with foil, place in the oven, and cook for 6 hours.

Remove from the oven and drain the juices into a large gravy separator. Slice the brisket thinly with an electric carving knife and pour the separated juices over the pieces. Serve with dinner rolls for brisket sandwiches au jus!

cornbread-chili casserole

1 tablespoon
vegetable oil

1 medium onion,
chopped

1½ pounds lean
ground beef

1½ cups mild salsa
(medium or hot
if preferred)

1 (11-ounce) can whole-
kernel white shoepeg
corn, drained

¼ cup vegetable stock

2 tablespoons hot
Mexican chili powder

1 teaspoon cumin

1 teaspoon salt

½ teaspoon freshly
ground black pepper

1 (7- or 8-ounce) box
cornbread muffin mix
(I like Jiffy)

½ cup whole milk

1 cup shredded
Cheddar cheese
(about 4 ounces)

¼ cup sour cream

When my nephew Kyle went away to college, although I know he loved his independence, I also know he had withdrawal from his mama's home cooking! When he comes to visit me, I never have to ask what he'd like me to cook. He never gets tired of this basic hearty casserole. It's easy enough for him to make himself, but don't tell him that, because then he might stop coming to see Aunt T!

SERVES 6

Preheat the oven to 375°F. In a large skillet over medium heat, heat the oil until shimmering, about 2 minutes. Add the onion and sauté until soft, 5 to 7 minutes. Add the ground beef to the onion, break up, and brown, 8 to 10 minutes. Drain any excess fat. Stir in the salsa, corn, stock, chili powder, cumin, salt, and pepper. Transfer the mixture into a 9 × 13-inch baking dish, smoothing into an even layer.

Mix the corn muffin mix with about ½ cup milk, or just enough to make it easy to spread. Spread it thinly over the chili mixture. Bake until browned on top, 30 to 35 minutes. Remove from the oven and set aside for 10 minutes to allow the casserole to set. Top with the Cheddar cheese and sour cream before serving.

Kyle and me at his high school graduation (2013).

karri's honey-marinated steak

¾ cup ketchup

2 tablespoons honey

¼ cup apple cider vinegar

3 garlic cloves, crushed

2 teaspoons onion powder

½ cup pineapple juice

1 teaspoon red pepper flakes

1 tablespoon natural mesquite-flavor liquid smoke

1 tablespoon cumin

2 teaspoons dried oregano

2 (1- to 2-pound) flank or skirt steaks or London broils

Salt and freshly ground black pepper

My friend Karri was in town from California visiting me one weekend when we got a call from my husband, who was on a plane heading home from Denver. He whispered into the phone, "I'm so sorry, but at this business meeting I was in today, in my excitement to make the deal happen, I promised everybody that you'd cook dinner for them. They're all on the plane with me. There will be twelve of us. Is that okay?" My answer was, "Sure, honey! Love ya! Bye!" I hung up and looked over at Karri, who was lying by the pool slathered in tanning oil just like me, and said, "Oh my! [Okay, what I really said isn't printable!] We have four hours to get dinner on the table and look fabulous!" I never would have made it without Karri! She told me about this easy steak marinade she liked to make, and off to the store we went. The steaks had only a couple of hours to marinate, but they were still delicious. When Garth and the guys walked in the door, salad was made, steaks were on the grill, and Karri and I were showered, dressed, and cute. No one was the wiser— except my husband, who still owes me! **SERVES 4**

Karri and me (2000).

In a small bowl, whisk together the ketchup, honey, vinegar, garlic, onion powder, pineapple juice, red pepper flakes, liquid smoke, cumin, and oregano. Pour the mixture into a shallow baking dish, then add the steaks to the dish and toss to coat.

Cover with plastic wrap and refrigerate for at least 2 hours or overnight. Remove from marinade, allowing the excess to drip off, and season with salt and pepper. Grill to desired doneness.

trisha tip

Less-expensive steaks like flank, skirt, or London broil need marinades to give them more flavor. They're the perfect cuts for this rich taste.

slow cooker georgia pulled-pork barbecue

PORK

2 medium sweet onions, quartered (I like Vidalia)

3 tablespoons firmly packed light brown sugar

1 tablespoon smoked paprika

2 teaspoons salt

½ teaspoon freshly ground black pepper

1 (4- to 6-pound) Boston pork butt roast

SAUCE

½ small onion

¼ cup water

1½ cups apple cider vinegar

¾ cup tomato juice

½ tablespoon freshly ground black pepper

1 teaspoon garlic powder

½ teaspoon cayenne

½ teaspoon hot sauce (I like Tabasco)

1½ teaspoons granulated sugar

trisha tip

Use disposable dishwashing gloves for applying the rub. It makes for an easy cleanup!

Everybody loves their region's barbecue. For me, growing up in middle Georgia, it was all about pulled pork. Even though I live in Oklahoma, where most of it is beef, I still prefer the sweetness of slow cooked pork. Luckily, our local barbecue hangout, Trail's End, serves it all, and their pulled pork reminds me of home. My dad was a great cook, especially when it came to barbecue, so I took inspiration from his pork recipe, and came up with a dish that I could slow cook all day. It's easy to put together, and the vinegar-based sauce tastes just like Daddy used to make!

SERVES 4 TO 6

To make the pork, place the onions in the bottom of a 5- to 6-quart slow cooker. Mix together the brown sugar, paprika, salt, and pepper and rub it all over the pork roast, then add to the slow cooker.

To make the sauce, chop the onion and puree it in a blender. You may need to add a drop of water to the blender to help the onion completely puree.

Place the pureed onion in a medium saucepan with ¼ cup of water to cover it. Bring to a boil over high heat, then reduce the heat to medium-low. Cook, stirring constantly, until the water has almost evaporated, about 5 minutes. Add the vinegar, tomato juice, pepper, garlic powder, cayenne, and hot sauce, and mix well. Increase the heat to medium-high, return

recipe continues

to a boil, then stir in the granulated sugar. Immediately remove the pan from the heat.

Drizzle 1 cup of the sauce over the roast in the slow cooker. Continue to cook the remaining sauce over low heat for 30 to 40 minutes, allowing it to reduce by half. Then remove the sauce from the heat, allow it cool completely for about 30 minutes, and refrigerate for later use.

Meanwhile, cook the roast in the slow cooker on low for 8 to 10 hours, checking after 8 hours for tenderness. Remove the meat and onions from the slow cooker. Discard the onions and finely shred the pork, using two forks. Reserve the juices from the slow cooker to add back to the meat for desired juiciness.

Serve on a bun with a little mustard. (I like to top my barbecue sandwich with coleslaw!)

Daddy cooking barbecue chicken for a crowd (1989)!

pork tenderloin with honey mustard glaze

1 tablespoon +
1 teaspoon grainy or
country Dijon mustard
(see Trisha Tip)

½ cup red wine vinegar

½ cup honey

3 garlic cloves, crushed

¾ teaspoon salt

Freshly ground black
pepper, to taste

3 tablespoons olive oil

1¾ pounds pork
tenderloin

We always had the same meal on New Year's Day. Mama would make a big batch of collard greens. The green leaves look like folded money, so they symbolized good fortune. Of course, she'd also make black-eyed peas, for luck, and pork, for prosperity. Most cultures serve some form of each of these dishes on the holiday. The pig symbolized progress, because he "pushes forward." Honestly, I don't really care why we eat it—I'm just glad we do! **SERVES 4**

Preheat the oven to 375°F. In a small bowl, whisk together the mustard, vinegar, honey, garlic, salt, pepper, and oil. Place the pork in a shallow baking dish and pour the glaze over the roast, turning to coat it.

Transfer the pan to the oven and roast the pork, basting it with the glaze occasionally, until the juices begin to thicken and the pork is cooked through, about 35 minutes. Remove the pan from the oven and allow the pork to rest for 10 minutes longer. Slice into ½-inch-thick slices.

trisha tip

Country Dijon is a milder, creamier version of Dijon. If you have trouble finding it, mix together 1 teaspoon of regular brown spicy mustard with 1 teaspoon mayonnaise.

pork, apricot, and rosemary kebabs

10 ounces apricot jam

2 tablespoons honey

2½ tablespoons country Dijon mustard (see Trisha Tip, page 97)

2 tablespoons low-sodium soy sauce

¼ cup olive oil

3 to 4 garlic cloves, crushed, plus 16 more for kebabs

Salt and freshly ground black pepper

3 to 4 branches of fresh rosemary

2 teaspoons freshly grated orange zest (about 2 oranges)

2 pounds pork tenderloin, cut into 1-inch cubes

3 tablespoons vegetable oil

8 (12-inch) metal or wooden skewers (see Trisha Tip)

Orange wedges, for garnish (optional)

trisha tip

If using wooden skewers, soak in a shallow dish of water for 15 minutes before using, to prevent splintering and to keep them from catching on fire during grilling.

My mama loved apricots! She introduced me to fresh, dried, and candied varieties. As a result, there's really no apricot that I won't eat. The sweetness of apricot jam in this pork marinade translates into sweet-and-sour pork, Trisha style. Getting those little rosemary sprigs on the skewer can be challenging, so feel free to crush the rosemary, put it in the marinade, and forget about it! You'll still get its essence in this easy dish. **MAKES 8 SKEWERS**

In a medium saucepan over medium-low heat, heat the jam until melted, about 2 minutes.

Transfer to a bowl. Add the honey, mustard, soy sauce, olive oil, crushed garlic and garlic cloves, ¾ teaspoon salt, pepper, rosemary, and orange zest, and mix until fully combined. Season the pork with additional salt and pepper and add to the marinade. Gently toss until coated. Transfer the mixture to a large sealable plastic bag and marinate in the refrigerator for at least 2 hours or overnight.

Heat a grill or grill pan to medium and lightly brush with the vegetable oil. Remove the pork, garlic cloves, and rosemary branches from the marinade, allowing the excess to drip off. Thread them in alternation onto the skewers, beginning and ending with pork. Grill the kebabs, turning occasionally, until the pork is cooked through, 12 to 14 minutes. Garnish with orange wedges, if desired.

sausage and peppers

5 medium red bell peppers, seeded and cut into 1-inch strips

2 large red onions, each cut into 8 wedges

6 garlic cloves, peeled

1½ pounds mild or hot sausage, cut on the diagonal into 2-inch pieces

1½ pounds Yukon Gold potatoes, cut into 1-inch pieces

¼ cup olive oil

My daddy was what I'd call a meat-and-potatoes man. He was a really good cook but liked to keep it simple. I can't think of anything simpler than hearty sausage combined with veggies and, of course, lots of potatoes! The apple (or potato) doesn't fall that far from the tree. I'm a meat-and-potatoes girl, too. Daddy and I also had in common that we liked spicy food, so pick your poison here, but I love the kick that the hot sausage brings to this dish. **SERVES 4**

Preheat the oven to 400°F. In a large bowl, gently toss the peppers, onions, garlic, sausage, and potatoes with the olive oil.

Transfer the mixture to a rimmed baking sheet and arrange in a single layer, working in batches or on multiple sheets as needed. Bake until the sausage is cooked through and the vegetables are tender, about 1 hour, gently tossing halfway through.

Beth grilling with Daddy (1964).

chicken, turkey & fish

Chicken Enchiladas

Chicken Tortilla Casserole

Chicken Saltimbocca

Individual Chicken Pot Pies

Broccoli Slaw Chicken

Raspberry Chicken

Unfried Chicken

Neat Sloppy Joes

Turkey-and-Dressing Casserole

Maple-Glazed Salmon

Citrus Cod Bake

Crab Cakes with Dill Tartar Sauce

Quinoa Corn Chowder

chicken enchiladas

4 boneless, skinless chicken breasts

2 tablespoons olive oil

¼ teaspoon freshly ground black pepper

½ teaspoon cumin

½ teaspoon dried oregano

1 package (2 teaspoons) taco seasoning

1 tablespoon salted butter

1 medium onion, chopped

1 (4-ounce) can chopped green chiles, with liquid

8 ounces cream cheese, softened

1 packet (1 ounce) of Hidden Valley Original Salad Dressing & Seasoning Mix

8 (8-inch) flour tortillas

16 ounces Monterey Jack cheese (about 4 cups), shredded

2 cups picante sauce

This is one of those quick go-to meals that I serve when we're craving Mexican food and I want it to be homemade. I usually cook a lot of chicken breasts at once and save them to use in various recipes throughout the week. If I don't have any on hand, I will buy a cooked rotisserie chicken and shred it into this dish. Supper is on the table in less than an hour, and everybody's happy! This yummy dish comes from Beth's friend Gail Shoup (of Chocolate Torte fame from Home Cooking with Trisha Yearwood*!). She lightened it up a bit by replacing heavy cream with picante sauce—and you'll never miss it!* **SERVES 4**

Preheat the oven to 350°F.

Spray a 9 ×13-inch baking dish with cooking spray and set aside.

Place the chicken breasts on a jelly roll pan. Drizzle ½ tablespoon of oil on each. In a small bowl, mix together the pepper, cumin, oregano, and taco seasoning, then sprinkle evenly over the chicken breasts.

Roast for 15 to 20 minutes on each side, or until golden brown and cooked through. Remove the pan from the oven, and allow to cool for 15 minutes. Shred the chicken and set aside.

Meanwhile, in a medium skillet set over medium heat, melt the butter until shimmering, about 2 minutes. Add the onion and sauté until soft, about 5 minutes. Add the green chiles and sauté for 1 minute. Stir in the cream cheese, dry ranch dressing mix, and the shredded chicken. Cook over medium

heat until the cream cheese melts, 3 to 5 minutes, stirring constantly.

Lay the tortillas flat on a clean, dry surface. Spoon 2 to 3 tablespoons of the chicken mixture into the center of each. Roll up the tortilla and place it seam-side down in the prepared baking dish. Sprinkle with the shredded Monterey Jack cheese. Pour the picante sauce over the rolled tortillas and cheese. Bake for 45 minutes, or until brown and bubbly.

chicken tortilla casserole

4 boneless, skinless chicken breasts

1 cup canned green chiles, chopped, and drained

1 medium onion, finely chopped

1 cup sour cream

½ teaspoon salt

¼ teaspoon freshly ground black pepper

½ teaspoon cumin

1 garlic clove, minced

2 cups Chicken Gravy (recipe follows)

24 (6-inch) corn tortillas

3 cups shredded Cheddar cheese (about 12 ounces)

My family has always loved casseroles. Garth especially likes the idea of getting the whole meal in one pan! If I'm going to be out of town for a day or two, I'll make this ahead and leave it in the refrigerator for him to warm up. You can substitute a can of cream of chicken soup for the chicken gravy, but it's really easy to make, and homemade always tastes better. Also, I love the crunch of the corn tortillas in this dish. **SERVES 8 TO 10**

Preheat the oven to 350°F.

Spray a 9 × 13-inch baking dish with cooking spray and set aside.

In a large stockpot over medium heat, add the chicken, cover with water, and bring to a boil. Cook until tender, about 30 minutes. Reserve 3⅓ cups stock (1 cup is for the chicken gravy), then remove the chicken from the pot and set aside to cool, about 20 minutes. Shred the chicken and set aside.

In a large saucepan set over medium heat, combine 2⅓ cups of the stock, green chiles, onion, sour cream, salt, pepper, cumin, garlic, and chicken gravy. Increase the heat to high and bring to a boil, stirring constantly. Remove the pan from the heat. Spread 1 cup of the mixture into the prepared dish. Arrange a layer of tortillas (about 6) over the mixture, then top with 1 cup of shredded chicken and ½ cup of cheese. Repeat these layers three more times, ending with cheese. Spread any remaining mixture over the top, then add the remaining cheese. Bake uncovered for 30 minutes.

CHICKEN GRAVY

6 tablespoons
salted butter

6 tablespoons
all-purpose flour

1 cup chicken stock

1 cup whole milk

1 teaspoon salt

¼ teaspoon freshly
ground black pepper

Melt the butter in a medium saucepan over medium heat, about 2 minutes. Whisk in the flour to make a roux. Cook over medium heat, whisking constantly, until the mixture bubbles and the flour browns lightly. Gradually whisk in the stock reserved from cooking the chicken and the milk, and continue to stir while cooking over medium heat. When the mixture thickens, whisk in the salt and pepper.

trisha tip

If you don't have enough stock from cooking the chicken, you can supplement with boxed chicken stock.

chicken saltimbocca

2 tablespoons
salted butter

2 tablespoons
all-purpose flour

1 cup chicken stock

1 tablespoon freshly
squeezed lemon juice

4 boneless, skinless
chicken cutlets

Salt and freshly ground
black pepper to taste

4 paper-thin slices
prosciutto

½ cup ricotta cheese

1 cup fresh spinach,
chopped

3 tablespoons olive oil

Saltimbocca is Italian for "jumps in the mouth." I can see how this dish got its name! This is one of those quick-to-assemble dishes that looks fancy. I love those! It's easy to make in bulk, so it's a great dish for parties. The chicken looks elegant on the plate, and your meal is fully cooked in no time. **SERVES 4**

In a medium saucepan set over medium heat, melt the butter, about 1 minute. Add the flour and whisk to make a roux. Cook until the flour browns slightly, about 1 minute. Add the stock and lemon juice and bring to a boil. Then reduce the heat and whisk constantly until thickened, about 5 minutes. Remove from the heat and set aside.

Place the chicken between two pieces of plastic wrap. Using a meat mallet or the heels of your hands, pound to evenly flatten to ⅛ inch in thickness. Remove the plastic wrap, and sprinkle on both sides with salt and pepper. Lay one slice of prosciutto on each piece of chicken, spread with ricotta, and top with spinach. Roll up each cutlet and secure with one or two toothpicks.

In a large skillet set over medium heat, heat the olive oil until shimmering, about 2 minutes. Add the chicken and sear until lightly browned, 2 to 4 minutes on each side. Add the sauce mixture to the skillet and bring the liquid to a boil. Reduce the heat to low, cover, and simmer for 10 minutes.

Transfer the chicken onto a serving platter. Remove the toothpicks from the chicken, and spoon the sauce over it before serving.

individual chicken pot pies

FILLING

2 boneless, skinless chicken breasts

3 large Yukon Gold potatoes, peeled and diced (about 2 cups)

½ cup (1 stick) salted butter

2 medium carrots, peeled and sliced

2 stalks celery, sliced

1 medium onion, finely diced

1 teaspoon salt

½ teaspoon freshly ground black pepper

½ cup all-purpose flour

1½ cups whole milk

1 cup frozen green peas

1 cup whole-kernel corn

¼ teaspoon celery seed

¼ teaspoon garlic powder

CRUST

2 cups baking mix (I like Bisquick) or self-rising flour (see Trisha Tip)

1 teaspoon freshly ground black pepper

1 cup (2 sticks) salted butter, melted

2 cups buttermilk (see Trisha Tip, page 202)

½ cup grated Parmesan cheese

The classic chicken pot pie has a crust on the bottom and on the top, so it usually involves a lot of rolling out dough. I'm all for finding the easier way! This simple biscuit-top crust makes putting this pot pie together a breeze. I love to serve it in individual ramekins because they're cute, and everybody gets their fair share of crust (which is the best part). If you prefer, it tastes just as amazing in one big 9 × 13-inch pan. **MAKES 8 INDIVIDUAL PIES**

Preheat the oven to 375°F. Grease eight 10-ounce ramekins with softened butter and place on a large rimmed baking sheet or jelly roll pan and set aside.

To make the filling, place the chicken in a large stockpot set over medium heat and cover with water. Bring to a boil and cook until tender, about 30 minutes. Remove the chicken from the pot, reserving the stock, and let cool for about 20 minutes. Then dice the chicken and set aside.

Put the potatoes into a medium stockpot set over medium-high heat and cover with water. Bring to a boil, and cook until the potatoes are tender, 15 to 20 minutes. Drain the potatoes in a colander and set aside.

Meanwhile, in a large saucepan over medium heat, melt 4 tablespoons of the butter, about 2 minutes, then add the carrots and cook for 5 minutes. Add the celery, onion, salt, and pepper. Cook until the onion is soft and almost

recipe continues

trisha tip

If you don't have self-rising flour, substitute 2 cups of all-purpose flour mixed with 3 teaspoons of baking powder and ¼ teaspoon of salt.

translucent, 4 to 5 minutes. Add the remaining 4 tablespoons of butter, and when it has melted, add the flour, stirring constantly to make a roux. Cook for 2 minutes until lightly browned, then add 3 cups of the reserved chicken broth and the milk. If you don't have enough reserved broth for 3 cups, supplement with boxed stock. Allow to simmer, stirring often, until the mixture thickens, 5 to 7 minutes. Stir in the peas, corn, chicken, celery seed, and garlic powder. Divide the cooked and drained potatoes evenly among the ramekins. Spoon the prepared filling into the ramekins, leaving about ½ inch of room at the top.

To make the crust, in a large mixing bowl, mix together the baking mix and the pepper until blended. Whisk in the melted butter, buttermilk, and Parmesan cheese until smooth.

Put ½ cup of the crust mixture on the top of each ramekin and smooth over, taking care not to mix it into the filling. Bake until the crust is crispy and brown, 40 to 45 minutes. Allow to sit for 10 minutes before serving.

broccoli slaw chicken

¼ cup olive oil

1 tablespoon salted butter

4 boneless, skinless chicken cutlets (thin, or pounded to equal thickness)

Salt and freshly ground black pepper

1½ cups of your favorite salsa or picante sauce

4 teaspoons hot sauce (I like Tabasco)

2 cups finely shredded broccoli

2 cups finely shredded carrots

2 cups finely shredded cabbage

trisha tip

The stovetop lid-on method of cooking chicken comes from *The Joy of Cooking* and is tried and true for skeptics like me, who are always worried the chicken isn't cooked through.

This easy chicken dish is full of protein and veggies. The hot sauce is optional, but it's what makes it so tasty to me! I usually double this batch when I know I'm going to have a busy week with little time to cook. I buy something called "broccoli slaw" at the grocery store. It's broccoli, carrots, and cabbage already shredded for you! So easy and so good. This is a great make-ahead meal that stores in the refrigerator for up to a week. All you have to do is reheat, and you're ready to go! **SERVES 4**

In a large skillet over medium heat, heat the oil and butter until shimmering, about 2 minutes, and swirl to coat the bottom of the pan. Season the chicken all over with salt and pepper, then add to the skillet and sear until lightly browned, about 2 minutes on each side. Add the salsa and hot sauce to the pan, coating the chicken. Cover the chicken with the shredded vegetables. Reduce the heat to low, cover, and allow to simmer for 10 minutes, then turn the stovetop off, keeping it covered. Allow to sit, with the heat off, to continue to steam the vegetables, and cook the chicken through for 10 minutes more.

raspberry chicken

4 boneless, skinless chicken breast cutlets

Salt and freshly ground black pepper

½ cup all-purpose flour

¼ cup olive oil

1 large shallot, thinly sliced

4 garlic cloves, finely chopped

½ cup white wine

1 cup chicken stock

6 ounces cremini mushrooms, sliced (about 3 cups)

1 cup fresh or frozen raspberries

1 teaspoon freshly grated lemon zest

2 tablespoons salted butter

1 tablespoon balsamic vinegar

Boneless, skinless chicken breast has been one of my go-to proteins in my quest to eat a more moderate diet, and it can get boring if I'm not creative. This raspberry chicken is so good—even though it's a newer addition to my recipe box, not a family recipe—I cook it so often it feels like I've been making it for years! Fresh raspberries can be expensive (and not always so fresh looking), so frozen are fine to use in this easy sauté. It's an elegant dish to share with company. I like to serve mine with a side of crisp green beans and fresh creamed corn. When I'm trying to drop a few pounds, I skip the breading step. You won't miss it, I promise! **SERVES 4**

Season the chicken with salt and pepper. Place the flour in a large, shallow bowl. Dredge the chicken in it and shake off any excess.

In a large skillet set over medium heat, heat the olive oil until it shimmers, about 2 minutes. Add the chicken and sear until slightly brown, 2 to 4 minutes on each side. Remove from the skillet and set aside. Add the shallot and garlic to the same pan and cook for 1 minute. Add the wine and stock, and cook until reduced slightly, about 10 minutes. Add the sliced mushrooms, reduce the heat to low, return the chicken to the skillet, cover, and cook for 10 minutes. Stir in the raspberries, lemon zest, butter, and balsamic vinegar.

Continue cooking, uncovered, until the butter melts, about 1 minute. If needed, add salt and pepper to taste. Transfer the chicken to plates and spoon the raspberry sauce and mushrooms over each piece.

unfried chicken

1 cup buttermilk (see Trisha Tip, page 202)

1 tablespoon hot sauce (I like Tabasco)

1½ cups multigrain panko bread crumbs

3 tablespoons grated Parmesan cheese

1 tablespoon freshly grated lemon zest

1 teaspoon red pepper flakes

Salt and freshly ground black pepper

4 boneless, skinless chicken breasts, cut in half

1 lemon, quartered

In adopting a healthier lifestyle, I've had to make some peace with my genuine love for fried chicken. I didn't give it up, but I'm down to eating it only a couple of times a year. This healthier unfried version of the South's favorite bird allows me to enjoy the comfort of fried chicken year-round, without all those added calories and fat! Buttermilk is lower in fat than whole milk and is a natural tenderizer for the chicken, too. **SERVES 4**

Preheat the oven to 400°F. In a medium shallow bowl, combine the buttermilk and hot sauce. In a separate medium shallow dish, combine the bread crumbs, Parmesan cheese, lemon zest, red pepper flakes, and a pinch of salt and pepper.

Season the chicken on both sides with salt and pepper and submerge in the buttermilk mixture. Remove, allowing the excess to drip off, then dredge in the bread crumb mixture, pressing to adhere. Lay the pieces flat on a nonstick baking sheet and refrigerate, uncovered, for 30 minutes. Then bake the chicken until crispy and brown, 20 to 25 minutes. Squeeze the lemon over the chicken before serving.

trisha tip

Don't skip the step of refrigerating for 30 minutes before baking. If you do, all of your "crust" will fall off. Don't ask me how I know!

neat sloppy joes

3 tablespoons olive oil

1 medium onion, finely diced

1 medium bell pepper, seeded and finely diced

1 pound ground turkey

1 (15-ounce) can fire-roasted diced tomatoes

1 (15-ounce) can kidney beans, drained and rinsed

¼ cup tomato paste

2 tablespoons apple cider vinegar

1 teaspoon firmly packed light brown sugar

Salt and freshly ground black pepper to taste

4 hamburger buns

There were very few times when my mama didn't cook supper for us, but when she fractured her foot and was laid up for a bit, Daddy was in charge of all cooking and cleaning duties. This was when he bought us a dishwasher—Mama had been asking for one for a while, but it took him having to wash the dishes himself to realize just how badly we needed it! Sloppy Joes were one of Daddy's signature dinners. I've lightened them up here by using lean turkey instead of ground beef.

MAKES 4 SANDWICHES

In a large skillet set over medium heat, heat the oil until it shimmers, about 2 minutes. Add the onion and bell pepper and sauté until softened, about 10 minutes. Add the turkey, breaking it up with a wooden spoon, and cook until browned, 5 to 7 minutes. Add the tomatoes, beans, tomato paste, vinegar, sugar, salt, and pepper, and cook for 5 to 10 more minutes or until heated through. Serve on hamburger buns.

trisha tip

You need to use olive oil to brown the turkey because the meat is so lean. As a result, you don't need to drain the meat before adding in the other ingredients.

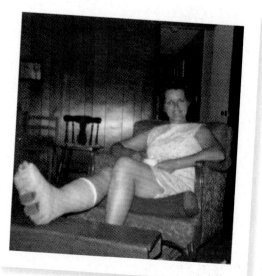

Mama with her broken foot (1973)!

turkey-and-dressing casserole

1 whole bone-in, skin-on turkey breast, 5 to 7 pounds

3 tablespoons unsalted butter, softened

Salt and freshly ground black pepper

1 teaspoon fresh rosemary, finely chopped

1 teaspoon fresh thyme, finely chopped

1 (8-inch) pan of prepared cornbread (about 1 pound), crumbled

10 slices white bread, torn into small pieces

¼ cup dried cranberries

2 tablespoons olive oil

4 celery stalks, finely chopped

2 carrots, peeled and finely chopped

1 medium onion, finely chopped

1 cup freshly squeezed orange juice

Chicken stock, for additional moistening of dressing, if needed

Here's the thing about Thanksgiving: We all have our own traditions. For me, it's the homemade cornbread stuffing my grandmother used to make—it's my favorite part of the meal. One year, my friends and I all found ourselves home for Thanksgiving without family coming into town (a rarity). We decided to get together and have our own "family" feast. Since we were creating a new tradition, I decided to depart from my tried-and-true turkey-and-dressing staples and make a casserole. Everybody loved it, and now I have something new to add to my holiday repertoire! **SERVES 6**

Preheat the oven to 325°F. Rub the turkey breast all over with the butter and sprinkle with salt, pepper, rosemary, and thyme. Place skin-side up in a large roasting pan and cover with a tight-fitting lid or aluminum foil. Bake until a thermometer inserted into the thickest part of the breast registers 165°F, 1½ to 2 hours, or about 15 minutes per pound.

Remove the turkey from the oven and allow to rest for 10 minutes. Cut into thick slices and set aside. Pour the pan juices into a measuring cup and skim off the fat, saving it to use for gravy.

In a large bowl, mix together the crumbled cornbread, torn white bread, and the cranberries. In a medium saucepan set over medium heat, heat the oil until it shimmers, about 2 minutes. Add the celery, carrots, and onion and cook until tender, about 7 minutes. Add ¼ cup of the turkey pan juices and continue cooking until the vegetables are translucent, about 6 minutes. Add the cooked vegetables to the bread mixture. Pour in the orange juice and 1 cup of the pan juices and mix well, using a sturdy spoon or your hands. Continue adding pan juices, supplementing with chicken stock as needed, until the mixture is very moist, almost soupy. Put the dressing in a 9 × 13-inch baking dish. Lay the turkey slices on top of the dressing. Cover the casserole and refrigerate overnight.

Preheat the oven to 350°F. Remove the casserole from the refrigerator and allow it to stand at room temperature while the oven is heating. Bake until warmed through, about 45 minutes. The dressing should be moist. If it appears to have dried out too much overnight, pour additional chicken stock over it.

maple-glazed salmon

2 tablespoons olive oil

2 tablespoons teriyaki sauce

¼ cup maple syrup

½ cup firmly packed light brown sugar

4 (6-ounce) salmon fillets

Sea salt and freshly ground black pepper

I know salmon is good for you—has omega-3s . . . blah, blah, blah—but I struggle to eat enough. Well, I have to say that Beth changed my mind about fish with this dish. Her friend Jana gave her this recipe and it changed "salmon night" forever at her house, becoming a family favorite. The teriyaki sauce, brown sugar, and maple syrup unite to give this dish a sweet, crispy vibe that has even me looking forward to salmon night. Bring on the omega-3s! **SERVES 4**

Preheat the oven to 400°F. In a small bowl, combine the olive oil, teriyaki sauce, maple syrup, and brown sugar. Whisk until fully combined.

Arrange the salmon, skin-side down, in a single layer in an 8 × 8-inch baking dish. Brush the glaze over the fish, coating evenly. Bake until the fish is cooked through but still bright pink inside, about 15 minutes. Season with salt and pepper to taste.

citrus cod bake

1 cup freshly squeezed orange juice

½ cup freshly squeezed lemon juice

3 to 4 green onions, thinly sliced

3 garlic cloves, crushed

½ cup olive oil

½ teaspoon red pepper flakes

2 pounds cod (about 4 fillets)

Salt and freshly ground black pepper

I admittedly am not a big seafood eater. It's mainly because, growing up in middle Georgia, "fresh seafood" was a misnomer! Most imported saltwater fish tasted too "fishy" to me. Our fresh fish consisted of what we caught in our spring-fed pond, which were mostly catfish and bream, or the occasional crappie. I learned to love saltwater crustaceans like crab and lobster when I visited coastal cities like Daytona Beach on summer vacations. I like mild fish best, so this citrus cod bake is perfect for me.

SERVES 4

trisha tip

Try this marinade on any other flaky white fish, like tilapia.

In a large plastic sealable bag, combine the orange juice, lemon juice, green onions, garlic, oil, and red pepper flakes. Season the fish fillets with salt and pepper on both sides, then add to the plastic bag, seal, and shake to coat. Lay the bag in the refrigerator for an hour, flipping halfway through to marinate the fish thoroughly on both sides.

Preheat the oven to 400°F. Cover a jelly roll pan with aluminum foil. Remove the fish from the marinade, allowing the excess to drip off, and place on the pan. Bake for 15 minutes, or until the fish flakes easily with a fork.

Daddy and his fresh catfish catch (1980).

crab cakes with dill tartar sauce

TARTAR SAUCE

¾ cup mayonnaise (I like Hellmann's)

3 tablespoons sweet relish

1 tablespoon chopped fresh dill weed

½ teaspoon salt

¼ teaspoon freshly ground black pepper

½ teaspoon white vinegar

CRAB CAKES

2 tablespoons salted butter, melted and cooled

2 large eggs

3 tablespoons sour cream

2 tablespoons coarsely chopped fresh parsley

1 teaspoon freshly grated lemon zest

2 tablespoons freshly squeezed lemon juice, plus wedges for serving

3 to 4 dashes hot sauce (I like Tabasco)

½ teaspoon Worcestershire sauce

1½ teaspoons Old Bay Seasoning

Even though I'm not a big seafood eater, I have always loved a good crab cake. There's really nothing like heading into a restaurant in a coastal town like Charleston, South Carolina, and having a fresh meal direct from the ocean right in front of you! I think I've tried every crab cake on the East Coast, from Key West, Florida, all the way up to Cape May, New Jersey, where I had some of the best king crab claws to go along with my seafood feast! The key is fresh lump crab meat. If you can't get it, just hold off until you can take a trip to Savannah, Georgia, or Myrtle Beach, South Carolina. It's worth the wait for the good stuff!

MAKES 12 CRAB CAKES

To make the tartar sauce, in a small bowl, combine the mayonnaise, relish, dill, salt, pepper, and vinegar. Cover and refrigerate for at least 30 minutes, or until ready to serve.

Meanwhile, in a large bowl, whisk together the melted butter, eggs, sour cream, parsley, lemon zest, lemon juice, hot sauce, Worcestershire sauce, Old Bay, capers, celery, and salt. Gently fold in the crab and bread crumbs. Form crab cakes by turning out ⅓ cup of the crab mixture for each cake onto a plate. Using the palm of your hand, lightly flatten the top to make patties.

In a large skillet over medium heat, heat the oil until shimmering, about 2 minutes. Cook the crab cakes in batches

1 tablespoon capers, drained and chopped

2 stalks celery, finely chopped

½ teaspoon salt, plus more for sprinkling

1 pound lump crab meat

¾ cup plain bread crumbs

¼ cup vegetable oil

until brown and crispy, 4 to 5 minutes per side. Transfer to a paper towel–lined plate to drain and sprinkle with salt. Serve with lemon wedges and a dollop of tartar sauce.

trisha tip

Try panko bread crumbs. They are Japanese bread crumbs made with crustless bread—a lighter version of traditional crumbs, which are made using the crusts.

quinoa corn chowder

2 tablespoons olive oil

2 tablespoons salted butter

1 medium onion, finely chopped

2 garlic cloves, finely chopped

1 cup golden quinoa

2 cups whole-kernel corn (or kernels from 2 to 3 large cobs)

5 cups chicken stock

½ cup heavy cream

1 2-pound bag of baby Yukon Gold potatoes, quartered

2 teaspoons Old Bay Seasoning

¼ pound (about 6 slices) bacon

1 pound medium shrimp, peeled and deveined

2 tablespoons fresh parsley, finely chopped

4 green onions, finely chopped

trisha tip

For those who like more spice, like me, add a touch of Tabasco or the hot sauce of your choosing to each serving.

When I discovered all the healthy facts about quinoa, I tried to find more ways to add it into my diet. Quinoa is called a supergrain because it's a complete protein, which means it contains all nine of the essential amino acids our bodies need. It has almost twice as much fiber as other grains and is loaded with iron, which every woman needs. I've always loved warm corn chowder on a cold day. I like this one as is but added the shrimp as an option for you seafood lovers out there! SERVES 4

In a large stockpot set over medium heat, heat the oil and butter, about 2 minutes. Add the onion and garlic, and sauté until tender, 5 to 7 minutes. Add the quinoa and corn, and sauté for 3 minutes more. Add the stock, cream, potatoes, and Old Bay. Increase the heat to high and bring the mixture to a boil, then reduce the heat to medium-low and simmer, uncovered, until the quinoa and potatoes are tender, about 30 minutes.

Meanwhile, using kitchen shears, cut the bacon into small pieces and add to a medium skillet set over medium heat. Cook until brown and crispy, about 4 minutes, stirring constantly. Remove to a paper towel–lined plate to drain. Set aside.

Add the shrimp to the quinoa and cook until they are pink and opaque, 2 to 3 minutes. Just before serving, add the parsley, green onions, and bacon.

Butternut Penne
(page 131)

pasta

Angel Hair Pasta with
Avocado Pesto
══════

Benita's Pasta Fazola
══════

White Wine Rotini
══════

Butternut Penne
══════

Tofu Ricotta Lasagna
══════

Peanut Butter Pasta

Julie's Pad Thai
══════

Pasta Primavera
══════

Easy Spaghetti
══════

Spaghetti Casserole
══════

Spinach-Stuffed Shells

angel hair pasta with avocado pesto

1 pound angel hair pasta

1 large bunch fresh basil leaves (about 3 ounces)

½ cup walnuts

2 ripe avocados, pitted and peeled

1½ tablespoons freshly squeezed lemon juice

4 garlic cloves

¼ cup olive oil

Salt and freshly ground black pepper to taste

Avocados are considered a source of good fat, so when I'm looking to add richness to a dish, it's my go-to fruit. It adds creaminess and color to this pesto, and the taste of the walnuts has this pasta bursting with flavor! **SERVES 6**

In a large stockpot, cook the pasta according to the package directions. Meanwhile, in a food processor, blend together the basil, walnuts, avocados, lemon juice, garlic, and oil. Add salt and pepper to taste.

Drain the pasta into a colander. Transfer it to a large serving platter or bowl and toss with the pesto. Serve immediately.

benita's pasta fazola

8 cups vegetable stock

12 ounces elbow macaroni

2 tablespoons olive oil

¼ cup finely diced onion (½ medium)

2 teaspoons minced garlic

1 (15-ounce) can fire-roasted diced tomatoes, with their juices

1 (15-ounce) can white beans (I like Great Northern), drained and rinsed

1 tablespoon dried oregano

Salt and freshly ground black pepper to taste

Grated Romano cheese, for garnish (optional)

My friend Benita is a vegan. She battled breast cancer and won! She strongly believes that an immune-boosting plant-based diet is a big part of keeping herself healthy, and I couldn't agree more. The challenge sometimes is finding dishes that are strictly plant based, without sacrificing great flavor. But Benita's really good at that balance, and this pasta fazola is the perfect example. To make this dish "Benita-approved," use egg-free noodles and don't add the Romano cheese at the end like I do. **SERVES 4**

In a large stockpot set over high heat, bring the vegetable stock to a boil. Add the macaroni and cook according to the package directions, then drain and set aside to cool, reserving the cooking stock.

Meanwhile, in a large saucepan set over medium heat, heat the oil until shimmering, about 2 minutes. Add the onion and garlic and sauté until softened, about 5 minutes. Add the tomatoes, beans, oregano, drained pasta, and reserved broth. Simmer for 5 minutes. Season with salt and pepper to taste.

Divide among plates and garnish with a little grated Romano cheese if desired.

white wine rotini

1 cup whole wheat panko bread crumbs

¼ cup Parmesan cheese

¼ cup + 2 tablespoons olive oil

3 teaspoons minced garlic

Salt and freshly ground black pepper to taste

8 ounces rotini pasta

2 medium sweet onions thinly sliced (I like Vidalia)

½ cup white wine

¼ cup vegetable stock

trisha tip

The skinny on cooking with wine: If you'd drink it, it's okay to cook with it. If you wouldn't drink it, don't use it in your recipes!

Beth makes this awesome pasta dish for her hungry men, and they love it. She's got two teenaged boys and a husband to feed, so she's always on the lookout for hearty, filling meals. This one fits the bill perfectly. Don't worry about the wine in the dish. The alcohol cooks out, so you just get the flavor, not the buzz! **SERVES 4**

Preheat the oven to 400°F. In a small bowl, mix together the bread crumbs, Parmesan cheese, 2 tablespoons of the oil, 1½ teaspoons of the garlic, and ½ teaspoon of salt. Spread in an even layer onto a baking sheet. Bake until golden brown, about 5 minutes. Remove from the oven and allow to cool.

Meanwhile, in a medium saucepan set over medium-high heat, cook the pasta according to the package directions, drain, and set aside.

In a large skillet set over medium heat, heat the remaining ¼ cup of oil until shimmering, about 2 minutes. Add the sliced onions and cook for 25 to 30 minutes, or until golden brown and caramelized, stirring occasionally. Add the remaining 1½ teaspoons of garlic and the wine. Cook until the wine reduces slightly, 2 to 3 minutes. Add the stock, and cook until the liquid reduces by half, about 5 minutes more.

Transfer the mixture to a serving platter or bowl and add the pasta. Season with salt and freshly ground black pepper and toss to combine. Sprinkle the bread crumb mixture on top for garnish.

butternut penne

1 pound penne pasta

¼ cup olive oil

1 medium onion, chopped

2 garlic cloves, finely chopped

1 pound butternut squash, peeled and diced into 2-inch pieces

¾ cup vegetable stock

3 tablespoons chopped fresh parsley

3 tablespoons salted butter, softened

½ cup grated Parmesan cheese

Salt and freshly ground black pepper to taste

I really do believe the key to eating healthier is to eat more of the good stuff and less of the bad stuff. Sounds pretty simple, but it's not so easy when the bad stuff tastes so good! The key is flavor. Butternut squash is one of my go-to vegetables because it has a great nutty flavor and it fills me up. If you want to make this pasta dish even healthier, you can leave out the butter altogether and use quinoa pasta. **SERVES 4**

In a large stockpot set over medium-high heat, cook the pasta according to the package directions. Drain and set aside, reserving a fourth of the cooking liquid.

In a large skillet set over medium heat, heat the oil until shimmering, about 2 minutes. Add the onion and sauté until soft and slightly browned, 5 to 7 minutes. Add the garlic and sauté for 2 minutes more. Add the squash and the stock, cover, and simmer until the squash is tender, about 15 minutes, stirring occasionally.

Return the pasta to the pot you cooked it in, and add the squash mixture. Add the parsley, butter, and Parmesan cheese, and season to taste with salt and pepper. Add as much or as little of the reserved pasta liquid until the sauce reaches your desired thickness.

tofu ricotta lasagna

1 (28-ounce) can fire-roasted diced tomatoes, with their juices

1 (12-ounce) can tomato paste

Salt

½ teaspoon freshly ground black pepper

¼ teaspoon garlic powder

1 tablespoon dried oregano

1 small onion, finely chopped

2 (15-ounce) cans black beans, drained and rinsed

1 tablespoon olive oil

8 ounces lasagna noodles

2½ cups Tofu Ricotta (recipe follows)

One of the things that Garth and I decided to do when we adopted a healthier lifestyle was try to make some meals that were meat- and dairy-free. This doesn't mean that we never eat those things—it just means that we try to do so less frequently. This black bean lasagna with tofu ricotta came about from that decision. I really had no experience with tofu, and I'm still on a learning curve, but what I know so far is that if I use it to replace something with similar feel and texture, it works for me. My family loves this meal, and we don't even miss the cheese—and for a cheese lover like me to say that is a big deal. Huge! You can even use whole wheat or quinoa lasagna noodles in this dish to make it that much healthier. **SERVES 8**

Preheat the oven to 375°F. In a large saucepan, combine the tomatoes, tomato paste, 2 teaspoons salt, pepper, garlic powder, oregano, onion, and black beans. Bring to a boil over high heat, then reduce the heat to low and simmer, uncovered, for about 30 minutes.

Meanwhile, bring a large pot of salted water to a boil over high heat. Add the oil, then add the lasagna noodles. Cook according to the package directions, drain, and set aside.

Spread 1 cup of the sauce in the bottom of a 9 × 13-inch baking pan. Then make three layers each of noodles, sauce, and tofu ricotta. End with an additional layer of sauce, and be sure the noodles are completely covered so they do not dry out during baking. Bake for 30 minutes, uncovered. Remove from the oven, and allow the dish to stand for 15 minutes before cutting into squares and serving.

trisha tip

Garth doesn't like his lasagna soupy AT ALL, but for more juiciness, you can add an 8-ounce can of crushed tomatoes to the sauce.

recipe continues

TOFU RICOTTA

MAKES ABOUT 2½ CUPS

¼ cup raw cashews, finely ground

14 ounces extra-firm tofu, drained (see Trisha Tip)

¼ cup nutritional yeast or grated Parmesan cheese

3 tablespoons olive oil

2 tablespoons finely chopped fresh basil

Salt and freshly ground black pepper to taste

This recipe was my first attempt at using tofu, and it was so incredibly, surprisingly tasty that it gave me confidence to try it in other dishes. Using quality olive oil and fresh basil in this cheese substitute makes it taste so fresh, it's like having your own cheese-making shop—much better than store-bought ricotta cheese, I promise! This awesome spread stores refrigerated in an airtight container for up to two weeks. It's great on top of your favorite pasta, or on a crunchy piece of melba toast as a snack.

trisha tip

To drain tofu, pour off any liquid from the block, then sandwich between two folded kitchen towels or several layers of paper towels on a plate or baking sheet. Place another plate or baking sheet on top and weight it with a heavy object, like a skillet or a book. Allow it to sit to drain.

Break drained tofu into small pieces. In a food processor, pulse the cashews until fine. Then add the tofu, nutritional yeast, oil, basil, salt, and pepper. Puree until fully combined.

peanut butter pasta

8 ounces angel hair pasta

¼ cup creamy peanut butter (I like Jif)

3 tablespoons sweet chili sauce

1 tablespoon low-sodium soy sauce

2 tablespoons freshly squeezed lime juice

½ cup finely chopped green onion

1 teaspoon red pepper flakes

⅓ cup olive oil

The first time I had peanut butter in pasta was in a little Thai restaurant in Nashville back in the early '90s. In Monticello, Georgia, peanut butter was strictly for pairing with grape jelly on a sandwich, or if you were feeling particularly adventurous, you might add it to frosting for your cupcake. But pasta? No way. One taste, and I was hooked on the sweetness of the chili sauce and the tanginess of the lime and the soy sauce, mixed in with the best flavor in the world (in my opinion). This recipe calls for creamy peanut butter, but I like to use extra-crunchy in my noodles. Yeah, peanut butter grows up. (Or maybe Trisha does!) **SERVES 4**

In a large stockpot set over medium-high heat, cook the pasta according to the package directions, then drain and set aside. In a medium bowl, whisk together the peanut butter, chili sauce, soy sauce, lime juice, green onion, red pepper flakes, and oil.

Transfer the noodles to a large serving dish. Toss with the peanut butter mixture and serve warm.

julie's pad thai

1 (14-ounce) package
dried thin rice noodles

1 tablespoon sugar

1 tablespoon fish sauce

¼ cup vegetable oil

1 block firm tofu, drained
and cut into 1-inch
cubes (see Trisha Tip,
page 140)

2 shallots, minced

2 large eggs

1 bunch green onions,
sliced

1 bunch bean sprouts

½ cup crushed peanuts,
for garnish

1 bunch radishes,
sliced, for garnish

2 limes cut into wedges,
for garnish

Chili powder, for garnish

Julie is one of my best friends. She really lives for her job, so when she took a vacation to Thailand a few years ago, I was proud of her for taking a rest for herself. When she came home and announced that she was adopting a little girl from an orphanage there, I was flooded with both surprise and delight. Julie brought home Intira, a gorgeous four-year-old. She immediately went to work trying to find as many things to help Intira adjust to her new environment while keeping as many traditions from her life in Thailand as possible. Julie came up with a version of pad Thai that they both love—and I love it, too! **SERVES 4**

In a large shallow dish, soak the noodles covered in water until pliable, about 10 minutes, then drain. In a small bowl, mix together the sugar and fish sauce and set aside.

In a large high-sided skillet or wok set over medium-high heat, heat the oil until shimmering, about 2 minutes. Add the tofu, turning until golden brown on all sides, 3 to 4 minutes, then transfer to a paper towel–lined plate to drain.

Using the same pan, sauté the shallots until translucent, about 1 minute. Add the eggs and break up while stirring together. Mix in the reserved tofu, fish sauce–sugar mixture, and the noodles, tossing to coat. Add in the green onions and sauté for another 30 seconds. Add the bean sprouts and remove the pan from the heat. Garnish with crushed peanuts, radishes, limes, and chili powder.

pasta primavera

1 pound spaghetti

¼ cup olive oil

1 medium onion, finely chopped

4 garlic cloves, minced

2 pints grape tomatoes, halved

1 pound asparagus, ends trimmed, stalks chopped into thirds

1 medium zucchini, quartered lengthwise then thinly sliced

¼ cup vegetable stock

1 large carrot, grated

¼ cup freshly grated Parmesan cheese

2 tablespoons freshly squeezed lemon juice

Salt and freshly ground black pepper to taste

¼ cup fresh basil, chiffonaded or torn into small pieces

I don't remember ever really eating "out" as kids. We lived in a small town, and the closest restaurant chain was an hour away, so Mama cooked at home almost every night. It helped that she was a phenomenal cook. Every supper was tasty and made with love. When I moved to Nashville, my mom and dad would come to visit, and I'd usually take them out to dinner as a treat. Mama fell in love with Olive Garden restaurants, and it became our "thing" when they'd come to town. She especially loved their pasta primavera, so this dish always makes me think of her. Primavera means "spring" in Italian, so traditionally this dish is made with fresh spring vegetables. I like the lightness of grape tomatoes and asparagus. **SERVES 4**

In a large stockpot set over medium-high heat, cook the spaghetti according to the package directions, drain, and set aside. In a large skillet set over medium heat, heat the oil until shimmering, about 2 minutes. Add the onion and garlic, and sauté until the onion is soft and translucent, 6 to 8 minutes. Add the tomatoes and cook until soft, 8 to 10 minutes more. Add the asparagus, zucchini, and stock.

Cover and cook for 8 to 10 minutes, until fork tender. Add the grated carrot and cook until heated through, about 2 minutes. Add the pasta, Parmesan cheese, and lemon juice. Season with salt and pepper to taste. Toss to combine. Garnish with the basil.

trisha tip

Chiffonade is a fancy way of saying slice into thin strips. It's a French term meaning "little ribbons." To chiffonade basil, stack four or five leaves on top of one another. Roll them into a tight cylinder. Cut along the cylinder widthwise. Unfurl and you've got thin strips.

easy spaghetti

1 pound thin spaghetti

¼ cup olive oil

4 garlic cloves, minced

3 cups grape tomatoes, halved lengthwise

Salt and freshly ground black pepper to taste

½ teaspoon red pepper flakes

¼ cup finely chopped fresh basil

¼ cup grated Parmesan cheese

I love Italian food, especially simple dishes made with fresh ingredients. There's nothing better than a simple pasta dressed with fresh basil, tomatoes, a little olive oil, and a touch of freshly grated Parmesan. It's almost too easy to be called a recipe. I call that perfection! **SERVES 4**

In a large stockpot set over medium-high heat, cook the spaghetti according to the package directions, drain, and set aside.

In a large skillet, combine the oil and garlic, then turn the heat to medium and sauté until golden and toasted, about 2 minutes. Add the tomatoes, salt, pepper, and red pepper flakes. Cover and cook until the tomatoes are softened, 5 minutes more. Add the basil, pasta, and Parmesan cheese, and stir to combine. Serve warm.

spaghetti casserole

8 ounces thin spaghetti

1 pound lean ground beef

1 medium green bell pepper, finely chopped

1 medium onion, finely chopped

1 (28-ounce) can crushed tomatoes

8 ounces cream cheese, softened

½ cup grated Parmesan cheese

8 ounces shredded mozzarella cheese

trisha tip

For a lower-fat version of this casserole, you can substitute ground turkey for the ground beef.

The first house I bought after I became a recording artist was a log cabin that sat atop a hill in north Nashville. My neighbor, who lived on the hill across the way, used to make a dish with leftover spaghetti noodles, and she'd always bring me some when I was home from the road. It was so nice to get off the bus knowing that she'd have something home cooked waiting for me! She pan-fried her noodles, but I've taken that idea and turned it into a casserole. It's a great way to use leftover spaghetti noodles, and, like most pasta dishes, it tastes even better the next day after the flavors have really had a chance to meld overnight. SERVES 6

Preheat the oven to 350°F. Spray a 9 × 13-inch baking dish with cooking spray and set aside.

In a large stockpot set over medium-high heat, cook the spaghetti according to the package directions, drain, and set aside. In a large saucepan set over medium heat, cook the ground beef, bell pepper, and onion until the ground beef is browned, 8 to 10 minutes. Drain any excess fat. Add the tomatoes and cream cheese to the pan, and stir until the cheese has melted into the mixture, 3 to 4 minutes.

Turn off the heat, then stir in the noodles and the Parmesan cheese. Pour the mixture into the prepared baking dish and bake, uncovered, for 25 minutes. Top with the mozzarella cheese and continue baking until the cheese has melted, about 3 minutes more.

spinach-stuffed shells

24 jumbo pasta shells (about 8 ounces)

2 teaspoons olive oil

1 medium onion, finely chopped

2 (15-ounce) cans crushed fire-roasted tomatoes

Salt and freshly ground black pepper to taste

2 cups baby spinach, finely chopped

1 cup Tofu Ricotta (page 140)

½ cup shredded mozzarella cheese, plus more for topping

1 egg, lightly beaten

This is a great pasta dish to make when you're having company. The jumbo pasta shells are elegant, and filling them with the creamy ricotta-spinach mixture makes them so pretty. People usually ooh and ahh when the pan comes out of the oven, because the dish just looks like it'd be labor intensive. I don't tell them otherwise! Even if you make your own homemade tofu ricotta, these are very easy to assemble. Throw in a little crispy garlic bread to scoop up anything that falls out of the shell, and you've got an impressive dinner! **SERVES 4**

Preheat the oven to 375°F. Spray a 9 × 13-inch baking dish with cooking spray and set aside.

In a large stockpot, cook the shells according to the package directions, then drain and set aside. Meanwhile, in a large saucepan set over medium heat, heat the oil until shimmering, about 2 minutes, then sauté the onion until browned, 5 to 7 minutes. Add the tomatoes and season with salt and pepper to taste. Reduce the heat to low and simmer for 10 minutes, then turn off the heat. In a large bowl, mix together the spinach, tofu ricotta, mozzarella cheese, egg, and a pinch each of salt and pepper.

Spoon half the tomato sauce into the bottom of the prepared baking dish. Stuff each shell with 2 tablespoons of the filling and place into the dish. Pour the remaining sauce over the shells, cover with aluminum foil, and bake for 30 minutes. Remove the foil, top with more mozzarella cheese, and return to the oven until the cheese is melted, about 5 minutes more. Remove the dish from the oven and allow it to stand for 10 minutes before serving.

Kyle's Grilled Zucchini
(page 163)

sides

Anita's Cheater Beans

Gwen's Coleslaw

Black Bean Quinoa

Brussels Sprouts with
Pistachios

"Go, Dawgs!" Greens

Smashed Sweet Pea
Burgers

Chickless Pot Pie

Mushroom Risotto

Kyle's Grilled Zucchini

Mama's Cornbread

Roasted Vegetables with
Balsamic Glaze

Grits-and-Greens
Casserole

South Tex-Mex Rice

Zucchini Cakes with
Herbed Sour Cream

anita's cheater beans

4 strips bacon, cut into ½-inch pieces

½ medium onion, finely diced

2 (27-ounce) cans pinto beans, drained and rinsed

2 serrano chiles, scored

1 medium tomato, finely diced

2 garlic cloves, minced

Salt and freshly ground black pepper

¼ bunch fresh cilantro, leaves only, snipped or pinched

trisha tip

Do not drain the bacon grease. It gives the beans a great flavor.

My friend Lory shared this recipe for the perfect side of beans. Her family of fabulous cooks hails from Del Rio, Texas, and they make everything from scratch. These beans are called "cheater" beans because Lory's Aunt Anita makes them without going through the time-consuming process of soaking dried beans. You'll never taste the difference, and you'll have this amazing dish on the table in no time! Lory calls this Mexican bean dish "Charro Beans" or "Frijoles Charros." **SERVES 6**

In a large saucepan over medium heat, fry the bacon until just cooked, about 6 minutes. Add the onion and cook until translucent, 6 to 8 minutes. Add the beans, chiles, tomato, garlic, and 1½ cups of water, and continue cooking until the vegetables soften, about 10 minutes. Add salt and pepper to taste, sprinkle in the cilantro, and cook for 1 minute. Remove the serrano chiles and discard.

gwen's coleslaw

2 cups cored and thinly sliced green cabbage (¼ small head)

2 tablespoons freshly squeezed lemon juice

¼ cup sweet relish

¼ small onion, sliced in half lengthwise and then crosswise into ¼-inch slices

1 tablespoon Dijonnaise

¼ cup mayonnaise (I like Hellmann's)

Salt and freshly ground black pepper to taste

For me, coleslaw usually conjures up images of big gatherings and huge serving bowls. Everybody's coleslaw is different; our "big" party version of this recipe includes shredded carrots, but my mama used to make this simpler coleslaw when it was just us—not a big crowd. I like how she snuck a little Dijonnaise in there for a subtle kick. This recipe makes only a couple of cups, but you can certainly do the math and make as much as you want if you're feeding a crowd! **MAKES 2 CUPS**

In a large bowl, mix together the cabbage, lemon juice, relish, onion, Dijonnaise, mayonnaise, salt, and pepper. Chill for at least 30 minutes before serving.

black bean quinoa

2 tablespoons olive oil

1 medium onion, finely chopped

4 garlic cloves, minced

1½ cups chicken stock

¾ cup red or golden quinoa

1 teaspoon ground cumin

¼ teaspoon cayenne pepper

Salt and freshly ground black pepper to taste

1 (11-ounce) can sweet corn kernels, drained

2 (15 ounce) cans black beans, drained and rinsed

¼ cup finely chopped fresh cilantro, for garnish

We've all heard about quinoa being a supergrain. It's not only good for you, it tastes good, too! This quinoa dish is a great side served with tacos or burritos. Garth likes to spread it over a layer of warm refried beans and use it as a dip for tortilla chips. Any way you try it, it rocks!

SERVES 6 TO 8

In a medium saucepan set over medium heat, heat the oil until shimmering, about 2 minutes. Add the onion and sauté until browned, 5 to 7 minutes. Add the garlic and sauté for 2 minutes more. Add the stock and quinoa and mix until fully combined. Add the cumin, cayenne pepper, salt, and pepper.

Increase the heat to high and bring the mixture to a boil. Immediately reduce the heat to low, cover, and simmer for 15 to 20 minutes, or until all the liquid is absorbed.

Remove the pan from the heat. Stir in the corn and black beans. Garnish with cilantro.

brussels sprouts with pistachios

1 tablespoon olive oil

1 shallot, finely chopped

1 pound Brussels sprouts, ends trimmed, halved

1 teaspoon freshly grated lemon zest

2 tablespoons freshly squeezed lemon juice

½ cup finely chopped shelled pistachios

Salt, to taste

My friend Ann is a great cook. When I go to her house for dinner, I always feel like I'm in an elegant restaurant, from the way she's set the table to the wine she's picked to the classy dinner she's prepared. Her dinners taste extravagant, but she swears they're easy to make. She proved it by sharing this recipe for pistachio-covered Brussels sprouts. She chops the ends off the sprouts and uses the leaves whole, but I'm too impatient, so I just halve them! Brussels sprouts sometimes get a bad rap for being bitter, but I love them. The lemon juice and the nutty crunch of pistachios are a nice addition to this underrated vegetable. **SERVES 4**

In a large skillet over medium heat, heat the olive oil until shimmering, about 2 minutes. Add the shallot and sauté until browned, about 3 minutes. Add the Brussels sprouts and sauté until just wilted, about 5 minutes. Add the lemon zest, lemon juice, and pistachios, and continue to sauté until completely heated through, 3 to 5 minutes more.

Remove the pan from the heat and top the Brussels sprouts. Season with salt to taste.

"go, dawgs!" greens

4 tablespoons olive oil

2 large bunches fresh collards, leaves removed and stems discarded, cut into 1-inch pieces

½ teaspoon salt

¼ teaspoon freshly ground black pepper

3 tablespoons sugar

2 teaspoons red pepper flakes

I love college football, especially my Georgia Bulldogs! Georgia fans are the ultimate tailgaters and know how to cook their collard greens. I got this recipe from Guy Thomson, owner of Proof of the Pudding catering company in Atlanta, and his executive chef, Vagn Nielsen, who provide the creative and delicious food for the suites at home games. I love the crunch of the sweet sugar with the savory flavor of the greens. They deserve our battle cry: "Go, Dawgs! Sic 'em! Woof! Woof! Woof!" **SERVES 4**

Beth and me at Sanford Stadium, Athens, Georgia (2012).

In a large skillet set over medium heat, heat 3 tablespoons of the oil until shimmering, about 2 minutes. Add the collards, salt, and pepper, and sauté until just al dente, about 15 minutes.

Remove from skillet and drain, reserving the cooking liquid, and transfer to a sheet pan to cool. Allow to air-dry, uncovered, refrigerated overnight. Refrigerate the reserved cooking liquid as well.

In a large skillet set over medium heat, heat the remaining oil until shimmering, about 1 minute. Add the collards and the sugar. Stir until the sugar begins to dissolve and the collards start to caramelize, about 15 minutes. Add some of the reserved liquid to help melt down the sugar as needed. Toss in the red pepper flakes, fully coating the collards before serving.

smashed sweet pea burgers

2 large sweet potatoes

2 (15-ounce) cans chickpeas (garbanzo beans), drained and rinsed

1 large egg, beaten

1 teaspoon chili powder

¼ cup all-purpose flour

Salt and freshly ground black pepper to taste

2 cups fine bread crumbs

½ cup finely grated Parmesan cheese

2 tablespoons olive oil

2 tablespoons butter

trisha tip

Mash the mixture together using a fork or pastry blender. Don't use a food processor or the burgers will be too mushy and won't hold together well for cooking.

There's not enough room on the page for me to name all the reasons that sweet potatoes are good for you. They are one of the best sources of beta-carotene, and they contain antioxidants and anti-inflammatory nutrients. That's just for starters! Maybe the most important characteristic of the sweet potato is that it tastes so yummy, however it's prepared. This crispy smashed version mixed with chickpeas is the ultimate veggie burger. Putting bread crumbs and Parmesan cheese in the mixture, along with the egg, really helps it hold together. I cook mine a little longer than this recipe suggests because I like them extra crispy. This burger tastes great on its own or on a toasted onion roll with honey mustard, lots of lettuce, and a slice of avocado. **MAKES 8 PATTIES**

Preheat the oven to 400°F. Pierce the sweet potatoes all over with a fork and bake on a fully lined baking sheet until soft, 60 to 75 minutes. Remove from the oven and allow to cool for about 20 minutes.

Halve the potatoes, scoop out the flesh into a medium bowl, and mash. Add the chickpeas and continue to mash. Mix in the egg, chili powder, flour, salt, pepper, bread crumbs, and Parmesan cheese until fully combined.

In a large skillet over medium heat, heat the oil and butter and swirl together, about 2 minutes. Using your hands, form the sweet potato mixture into 8 patties. Add to the pan and cook until brown and crispy, 4 to 5 minutes per side, working in batches as needed. Transfer to a paper towel–lined plate to drain.

chickless pot pie

½ cup (8 tablespoons) Earth Balance Buttery Spread

1 cup peeled carrots, sliced into ½-inch slices

1 cup frozen green peas

½ cup sliced celery

1 cup red potatoes, peeled and diced into ½-inch cubes

⅓ cup finely chopped onion

⅓ cup all-purpose flour

½ teaspoon salt

¼ teaspoon freshly ground black pepper

¼ teaspoon celery seed

¼ teaspoon garlic powder

1¾ cups vegetable stock

⅔ cup almond or soy milk

2 (9-inch) deep-dish unbaked piecrusts (I like Mrs. Smith's)

This recipe was completely inspired by my mom. In her battle with breast cancer, she chose to take all meat and dairy out of her diet, but she didn't want to give up flavor, and she especially didn't want to give up those comfort foods she loved. She came up with this pot pie that is so delicious, but completely cholesterol-free! I'm certainly not an expert on the best way to eat, but I know getting nutrition from vegetables is a good thing. **SERVES 8**

Preheat the oven to 425°F.

In a medium saucepan set over medium heat, melt 3 tablespoons of the Earth Balance. Add the carrots, peas, and celery, and sauté for five minutes or until slightly soft. Add the potatoes, cover with water, increase the heat to high and bring to a boil. Cook until the potatoes are fork tender, about 15 minutes. Drain the vegetables and set aside.

In the same saucepan, over medium heat, melt the rest of the Earth Balance, about 2 minutes, then sauté the onion until it is soft and translucent, 5 to 7 minutes. Stir in the flour, salt, pepper, celery seed, and garlic powder. Cook until the flour browns slightly, about 2 minutes. Slowly stir in the stock and the almond milk. Reduce the heat to medium-low, and simmer until thickened, about 5 minutes.

Remove the saucepan from the heat and stir in the vegetables. Pour the mixture into the bottom crust. Cover with the second crust, pinch the edges to seal, and cut small slits in the top to allow steam to escape.

Bake until the pastry is golden brown and the filling is bubbly, 30 to 35 minutes. Remove from the oven and allow to cool for 10 minutes before serving.

Beth, Mama, and me (2009).

mushroom risotto

5 tablespoons olive oil

3 shallots, finely diced

½ pound (1 cup) mushrooms, sliced

2 garlic cloves, finely chopped

2 cups arborio rice

Salt and freshly ground black pepper to taste

1 cup white wine

6 cups chicken stock

1 tablespoon freshly squeezed lemon juice

3 tablespoons grated Parmesan cheese

¼ cup heavy cream

2 tablespoons salted butter

trisha tip

For a faster cooking time, warm the chicken stock in a medium saucepan before adding it into the risotto.

This is one of Garth's favorite meals, though he can never pronounce it correctly! I guess we've been together long enough that I'm a good interpreter, because I always seem to know what he means when he's asking for it. This is one of those dishes I make with a lot of love, because it takes time and a lot of stirring! It's most definitely worth it, though, because my cowboy always has a smile on his face and a big "thank you" when I make it for him. I am usually smiling, too, because he says it's the best "rozooti" he's ever tasted! **SERVES 6**

In a large stockpot set over medium heat, heat the oil until shimmering, about 2 minutes. Sauté the shallots and mushrooms until softened, 5 to 7 minutes. Add the garlic and sauté until fragrant, 1 more minute. Add in the arborio rice and a pinch of salt. Sauté for 2 minutes. Then add the wine and cook until the liquid is absorbed, 4 to 5 minutes. Add the stock 1 cup at a time, stirring after each addition until all of the liquid is absorbed. Season periodically with salt and pepper to taste. (This process takes about 30 minutes of constant stirring.)

Remove the pan from the heat. Stir in the lemon juice, Parmesan cheese, cream, and butter. Serve with your favorite crusty bread.

kyle's grilled zucchini

½ cup kosher salt

1½ teaspoons dried oregano

1½ teaspoons dried thyme

3 large zucchini, thinly sliced lengthwise

Olive oil, for brushing

½ cup crumbled feta cheese

trisha tip

Store the herb salt in an airtight container for up to a year.

Since becoming a college kid, my nephew Kyle has started to learn the value of cooking. Grilled zucchini is his "thing." He makes this herb salt and sprinkles a little on the zucchini before grilling, saving the rest for other uses. I don't know how his grades are gonna be this semester, but he gets an A in grilling from Aunt T! **SERVES 6**

In a medium bowl, mix together the salt with the oregano and thyme. Brush both sides of the zucchini slices with olive oil, and sprinkle with a little of the herb salt mixture. Place on a hot outdoor grill or a grill pan over medium heat. Cook for 10 minutes, flipping halfway through. Remove from the heat, transfer to a serving platter, and sprinkle with the feta cheese.

mama's cornbread

1 teaspoon apple cider vinegar

1½ cups unsweetened almond milk

4 tablespoons canola oil

2 cups self-rising cornmeal mix

1 large egg white, lightly beaten

½ cup whole-kernel corn, drained (or kernels off one cob)

¼ cup seeded and chopped jalapeños (optional)

trisha tip

To prevent sticking, cut a circle of aluminum foil to line the bottom of the pan before greasing it. When baked, turn the bread out on a cooling rack and peel off the foil.

Mama and Beth (1962).

One of the things I admired most in my mama was her never-ending interest in learning and trying new things. I am not overstating when I say she was a great cook, so in my mind, she didn't need to try to improve upon anything she made. She knew how to make things taste better, and she always knew how to fix something if it went wrong—in the kitchen and in life! I shouldn't have been surprised when she decided to take the cornbread recipe that she'd been making with her own mother since she was a little girl and revamp it into something a bit lighter. (Our original version includes bacon drippings and lots of corn oil!) Even into her seventies, she was hungry for knowledge in all things and knew there was always something new to discover. I think I'm more set in my ways than she was, but I aspire to be more like Gwen every day. **MAKES 8 SLICES**

Preheat the oven to 450°F.

In a 2-cup measuring cup, add the vinegar to the milk and set aside to curdle.

Add 2 tablespoons of the oil to a 9-inch cast-iron skillet set over medium heat, and heat until shimmering, about 2 minutes.

In a large bowl, mix together the cornmeal mix, the remaining oil, and the vinegar-milk mixture. Stir in the egg white, corn, and jalapeños, if using. Pour the cornmeal mixture into the skillet, listening for a sizzle. Some of the oil will come up around the edges. Smooth it over the top of the mixture. Bake until lightly browned, 20 to 25 minutes.

roasted vegetables with balsamic glaze

VEGETABLES

½ pound carrots, peeled and cut on the diagonal into 1-inch slices

1 head of garlic, cloves removed

½ pound Brussels sprouts, ends trimmed and halved

2 sweet potatoes, peeled and cut into 1-inch pieces

½ pound fingerling potatoes, halved

1 medium butternut squash, peeled and diced

2 large sweet onions, peeled and cut into quarters

¼ cup olive oil

1 teaspoon salt

½ teaspoon freshly ground black pepper

GLAZE

¼ cup balsamic vinegar

2 tablespoons honey

2 teaspoons country Dijon mustard (see Trisha Tip, page 97)

⅓ cup vegetable stock

½ cup olive oil

1 teaspoon freshly squeezed lemon juice

Salt and freshly ground black pepper to taste

When my friend Donna comes over, she always brings something, whether it's an awesome salad or a great bottle of wine. She and I love these roasted vegetables, and she always makes the glaze. She doesn't have a recipe for it, just makes it up as she goes along from whatever she can find in my kitchen. Her original concoction had balsamic vinegar, mustard, and leftover Italian dressing. Now we make our own! **SERVES 6**

Preheat the oven to 400°F.

In a large bowl, toss the vegetables in extra-virgin olive oil and sprinkle with salt and pepper. Spread in an even layer onto a large jelly roll pan. Roast until tender, 35 to 40 minutes, stirring once.

Meanwhile, in a small saucepan, combine the balsamic vinegar, honey, Dijon, stock, oil, lemon juice, salt, and pepper. Cook over low heat until the glaze is reduced by half, about 10 minutes. Pour the glaze over the vegetables, or serve on the side as a dipping sauce.

grits-and-greens casserole

2 cups half and half

8 cups chicken stock

2 cups grits (I like Quaker Aunt Jemima Old Fashioned)

6 slices bacon

1 medium sweet onion, finely chopped (I like Vidalia)

1 (16-ounce) package fresh or frozen collard greens

½ cup (1 stick) salted butter

1¾ cups (6 ounces) grated Parmesan cheese

1 teaspoon salt

½ teaspoon freshly ground black pepper

8 ounces Monterey Jack cheese, shredded

What could possibly be more southern than grits and collard greens? I love them both so much! Imagine my delight at finding a way to combine them in one creamy dish! Even confirmed "grits-haters" have given it a thumbs-up. And while longtime fans of the humble grit draw the line at leftovers, this casserole is just as good warmed up as it is right out of the oven. Grits—they're not just for breakfast anymore! **SERVES 8 TO 10**

Preheat the oven to 350°F. Spray a 9 × 13-inch baking dish with cooking spray and set aside.

In a large pot or dutch oven set over medium-high heat, bring the half and half and 6 cups of the chicken stock to a boil. Stir in the grits and return them to a boil. Then reduce the heat to low, cover, and simmer until the grits have thickened slightly, 10 to 15 minutes, stirring frequently. Use a whisk to break up any lumps.

trisha tip

Don't use instant or quick-cooking grits for this dish. Use old-fashioned raw grits. When cooked, they are lump-free and resemble oatmeal in thickness.

Uncle Wilson, Mama, and Beth in his collard patch (2008).

Meanwhile, using kitchen shears, cut the bacon into small pieces and, in a large saucepan set over medium heat, cook until just crispy, about 7 minutes. Using a slotted spoon, remove the bacon and transfer to a paper towel–lined plate to drain. Add the onion to the bacon drippings in the pan and sauté until tender, 5 to 7 minutes. Add the collard greens and the 2 remaining cups of chicken stock and cook until tender, about 10 minutes. Drain the collards and onion.

When the grits are done, add the butter, Parmesan cheese, salt, pepper, and ½ cup of the shredded Monterey Jack cheese to the grits, and stir until combined and melted. Add the collard green mixture and stir. Transfer the mixture to the prepared baking dish and top with the crumbled bacon and the remaining ½ cup of Monterey Jack cheese. Bake until the cheese is melting and bubbly, about 15 minutes.

south tex-mex rice

3 tablespoons vegetable oil

2 cups long-grain rice

4 cups vegetable stock

1 large onion, diced

1 large tomato, diced

½ bunch cilantro, whole leaves torn

1 large green bell pepper, seeded and deveined, diced

4 fresh serrano chiles, scored

1 tablespoon cumin

2 teaspoons minced garlic

2 teaspoons salt

1 teaspoon freshly ground black pepper

Growing up, the only things I ever put on rice were butter and gravy. I never knew long-grain white rice could be bursting with this kind of flavor! My friend Lory has been making this rice her whole life. Her mama taught her how to make it, but she never used a recipe. I told her she had to write it down for me so I could share it with all of you! Serrano chiles are hotter than jalapenõs. Scoring them allows the spice to seep into the rice, but don't forget to remove the peppers before serving. You really don't want to bite into one! **SERVES 6 TO 8**

In a large skillet set over medium heat, heat the oil until shimmering, about 2 minutes. Add the rice and cook, continually stirring, until lightly browned, taking care not to burn it, 10 to 15 minutes.

Add the stock (it will make a loud sizzling noise, so stand back a bit), the onion, tomato, cilantro, bell pepper, chiles, cumin, garlic, salt, and pepper. Increase the heat to high and bring to a boil. Taste the juice with a spoon and season to your liking.

Reduce the heat to low, cover, and simmer for 15 minutes. (Do not uncover during cooking.) Remove the chiles and discard. Fluff and serve.

zucchini cakes with herbed sour cream

3 cups shredded zucchini (about 2 large zucchini)

2 cups panko bread crumbs

¼ cup grated Parmesan cheese

1 teaspoon minced garlic

2 teaspoons fresh oregano, finely chopped

2 teaspoons fresh basil, finely chopped

1 teaspoon salt, plus more for sprinkling

½ teaspoon freshly ground black pepper

4 large eggs

½ cup buttermilk (see Trisha Tip, page 202)

¼ cup olive oil

Herbed Sour Cream (recipe follows)

trisha tip

Substitute 1 cup of Egg Beaters for the eggs. Same great taste, but no cholesterol.

Zucchini is one of those magic vegetables that can adapt to a lot of different dishes well. I like it simply sautéed, lightly cooked in pasta primavera, even finely shredded lengthwise and boiled to use in place of spaghetti noodles. Mixed with bread crumbs and spices and pan-fried into a crispy cake is my new zucchini specialty! Beth's friend Kelli shared this awesome recipe. It's great alongside any meal, but I especially like it for breakfast, maybe because these crispy cakes have the consistency of potato pancakes. The herbed sour cream is a nice cool complement. **MAKES 8 TO 10 ZUCCHINI CAKES**

In a large bowl, mix together the zucchini, bread crumbs, Parmesan cheese, garlic, oregano, basil, the 1 teaspoon of salt, and pepper. In a separate medium bowl, whisk the eggs together with the buttermilk. Then stir the egg mixture into the zucchini mixture.

In a large skillet set over medium heat, heat the oil until shimmering, about 2 minutes. Using your hands, form the zucchini mixture into 8 to 10 patties (about ¼ cup for each patty) and add to the pan. Pan-fry the cakes, working in batches as needed, until golden brown, about 3 to 5 minutes per side. Transfer to a paper towel–lined plate to drain, sprinkle with salt, and serve hot and crisp with herbed sour cream.

HERBED SOUR CREAM

2 cups sour cream

1 tablespoon chopped fresh chives

1 tablespoon chopped fresh dill weed

In a medium bowl, whisk together the sour cream, chives, and dill.

Lemon Poppy Seed Cake
(page 187)

cakes, cupcakes & pies

1-2-3-4 Pound Cake with Apple, Pear, and Plum Compote

Chocolate Orange Cake

Banana Pudding Cake

Basic Cupcakes with Peanut Butter Frosting

Chocolate Angel Food Cake with Strawberries

Hawaiian Cake

Lemon Poppy Seed Cake

Key Lime Cheesecake with Raspberry Sauce

Texas Sheet Cake with Chocolate Ganache

Kiwi Lime Pie

Boston Cream Pie

Mrs. Carter's Skillet Apple Pie

1-2-3-4 pound cake with apple, pear, and plum compote

¾ cup + 2 tablespoons solid vegetable shortening (I like Crisco)

2 cups sugar

4 large eggs, at room temperature

1 teaspoon vanilla extract

2 tablespoons freshly grated lemon zest

3 cups all-purpose flour

4 teaspoons baking powder

¾ teaspoon salt

1 cup whole milk

Apple, Pear, and Plum Compote (recipe follows)

My mama made cakes for a living before Beth and I were old enough to go to school. She had been a teacher, but she took that time to be home with us and earned some extra money for the family by making everything from birthday cakes to wedding cakes! She had some amazing creations. Her standard birthday cake was this lighter version of the usual pound cake. If you've ever watched the movie Steel Magnolias, *you've heard about the "cuppa, cuppa, cuppa" cake. (If you haven't ever seen this movie, put this book down right now, and go watch it. I'm* not *kidding!) This is the Yearwood variation, which is really a "cuppa, 2 cuppa, 3 cuppa, 4 cuppa" cake! It's an easy recipe and makes a light cake. Top with Apple, Pear, and Plum Compote and enjoy!* **SERVES 12**

Preheat the oven to 325°F. Spray a 9 × 5-inch loaf pan with cooking spray and set aside.

Using the large bowl of an electric mixer fitted with the paddle attachment, cream the shortening and sugar until light and fluffy, about 5 minutes. Add the eggs, one at a time, beating well after each addition. Add the vanilla and lemon zest. Sift the flour, baking powder, and salt together on a sheet of waxed paper, then add the flour mixture to the butter

recipe continues

mixture in batches, alternating with the milk and beginning and ending with the flour.

Pour the batter into the prepared pan and bake for 40 minutes, or until a toothpick inserted in the cake comes out clean. Remove from the oven and cool in the pan for 5 minutes, then turn out onto a rack to cool completely, about 20 minutes. Top with each slice with fruit compote before serving.

APPLE, PEAR, AND PLUM COMPOTE

MAKES 2 CUPS

2 cups peeled Granny Smith apples (about 2 medium), cut into 1-inch cubes

2 cups ripe firm pears (about 2 medium), cut into 1-inch cubes (I like Bosc)

2 cups diced plums (about 3 large)

½ cup water

¼ cup honey

½ teaspoon vanilla extract

½ teaspoon ground cinnamon

In a large saucepan, combine the apples, pears, plums, water, honey, vanilla, and cinnamon. Bring to a boil over high heat, reduce the heat to medium-low, cover, and simmer until the fruits begin to soften, about 20 minutes. Uncover and continue cooking until the syrup is reduced and the fruit is tender, 20 to 25 minutes. Remove from the heat, and allow to cool completely. May be served cold, or warmed before topping cake.

chocolate orange cake

CAKE

½ cup unsweetened cocoa powder, plus more for dusting the pan

3 cups all-purpose flour

1½ cups granulated sugar

2 teaspoons baking soda

1 teaspoon salt

1 teaspoon ground cinnamon

¾ cup mayonnaise (I like Hellmann's)

1 teaspoon vanilla extract

2 tablespoons balsamic vinegar

2 cups freshly squeezed orange juice

2 tablespoons freshly grated orange zest

GLAZE

1 cup confectioners' sugar (see Trisha Tip, page 207)

2 tablespoons unsweetened cocoa powder

3 tablespoons freshly squeezed orange juice

You know those chocolates that you crack open and they look like orange sections, only they're chocolate, flavored with the fruit? This cake gives me that combination I love. The key is to use just enough juice in the glaze to make it pourable, but not too thin. Don't be afraid to experiment until you get it just right. **SERVES 12**

Preheat the oven to 350°F. Spray a Bundt pan with cooking spray, then lightly dust with cocoa powder and set aside.

Using an electric mixer, combine the flour, granulated sugar, baking soda, salt, cocoa powder, and cinnamon and mix until blended. Add the mayonnaise, vanilla, vinegar, and orange juice and mix until just combined, 1 to 2 minutes. Fold in the orange zest.

Pour the batter into the prepared pan and bake for 45 minutes, or until a toothpick inserted near the center comes out clean. Remove from the oven and allow to cool in the pan for 10 minutes, then turn out onto a rack to cool completely.

To make the glaze, mix the confectioners' sugar and the cocoa powder together. One tablespoon at a time, whisk the orange juice into the dry mixture until it reaches a good consistency to drizzle. Test it by dipping a fork into the glaze, pulling it out, and letting it run back into the bowl. Drizzle the glaze over the completely cooled cake.

banana pudding cake

CAKE

1½ cups ripe bananas (2 large bananas)

2 teaspoons freshly squeezed lemon juice

¾ cup (1½ sticks) salted butter, softened

2 cups granulated sugar

3 large eggs, at room temperature

1 (11-ounce) box vanilla wafers, crushed

1 cup buttermilk (see Trisha Tip, page 202)

2 teaspoons vanilla

FILLING

¼ cup granulated sugar

1 tablespoon all-purpose flour

1 tablespoon cornstarch (see Trisha Tip, page 193)

Pinch of salt

1 large egg + 1 yolk

1 cup whole milk

¼ teaspoon vanilla extract

Confectioners' sugar, for sprinkling

This recipe was inspired by a cake my grandmother Yearwood used to make. She substituted crushed vanilla wafers for flour. I took her genius idea and my love for banana pudding, and came up with a cake that has all the flavors I love. Thanks, Grandma! **SERVES 12**

Preheat the oven to 350°F. Spray two 9-inch round cake pans with cooking spray, lightly dust with flour, and set aside. In a small bowl, mash the bananas, then stir in the lemon juice.

Using an electric mixer, cream the butter and granulated sugar until fluffy, about 5 minutes. Add the eggs, one at a time, beating well after each addition. Add the crushed vanilla wafers in batches, alternating with the buttermilk and beginning and ending with the wafers. Add the mashed bananas and vanilla, and beat until fully incorporated.

Divide the batter evenly between the prepared pans and bake for 1 hour and 15 minutes, or until a toothpick inserted in the center comes out clean. Remove the cakes from the oven and cool in the pans for 10 minutes, then turn out on racks to cool completely, about 20 minutes.

To make the filling, in the top of a double boiler, whisk together the granulated sugar, flour, cornstarch, and salt. Stir in the whole egg plus the yolk, then stir in the milk. Cook, uncovered, stirring often, until the mixture thickens, about 10 minutes. Remove from the heat and stir in the vanilla. Allow to cool completely, about 15 minutes, then spread between the cooled cake layers.

Chill the cake in the refrigerator to allow the pudding filling to set, 30 minutes to 1 hour. Top with confectioners' sugar before serving.

trisha tip

If you don't have a double boiler, make your own! All you need is a saucepan filled with about an inch of water and a heatproof bowl that fits a couple of inches above the saucepan's base. Be sure it fits tightly on top of the saucepan. Add your ingredients, then cook over high heat, bringing the water to a boil. The heat from the constant steam will cook the filling without scorching.

Grandma Yearwood and Beth (1962).

basic cupcakes with peanut butter frosting

CUPCAKES

1½ cups granulated sugar

½ cup (1 stick) salted butter, softened

2 large eggs, at room temperature

3 cups cake flour, sifted

2 teaspoons baking powder

½ teaspoon salt

1¼ cups whole milk

1½ teaspoons vanilla extract

FROSTING

½ cup (1 stick) salted butter, softened

1 cup creamy peanut butter

3 cups confectioners' sugar (see Trisha Tip, page 207)

¼ cup whole milk, plus more if needed

1 teaspoon vanilla extract

If you make homemade vanilla cupcakes, you probably have a recipe very similar to this one. Every cupcake baker I know follows a version of this tried-and-true moist cupcake. I grew up eating either buttercream or chocolate frosting on cupcakes. Don't get me wrong, they were awesome, but once I discovered peanut butter frosting, my life was changed forever. I cannot speak enough to my love affair with peanut butter. It's good on everything, from cupcakes to bacon cheeseburgers—yep, I said bacon cheeseburgers! **MAKES 12 CUPCAKES**

Preheat the oven to 350°F. Fill a 12-count muffin tin with liners and set aside.

Using an electric mixer, cream together the granulated sugar and butter until fluffy, about 5 minutes. Add the eggs one at a time, beating well after each addition. On a sheet of waxed paper, sift the flour, baking powder, and salt together, then add the flour mixture to the butter mixture in batches, alternating with the milk and beginning and ending with the flour. Add the vanilla and mix until the batter is smooth.

Divide the batter evenly among the prepared muffin tin cups, leaving an ⅛-inch space at the top of each. Bake for 18 to 20 minutes, or until a toothpick comes out clean. Turn the cupcakes out onto a rack to cool completely, about 15 minutes.

Meanwhile, to make the frosting, using an an electric mixer, beat the butter and peanut butter together until fluffy,

about 5 minutes. Slowly add 1½ cups of the confectioners' sugar, ¼ cup of the milk, and the vanilla until combined. Beat in the remaining confectioners' sugar. Add additional milk 1 tablespoon at a time until the frosting is a creamy, spreadable consistency.

Generously frost the cupcakes.

trisha tip

For even richer frosting, use heavy cream instead of milk and replace half of the creamy peanut butter with extra-crunchy peanut butter.

chocolate angel food cake with strawberries

¾ cup sifted cake flour

¼ cup unsweetened cocoa powder

1¾ cups sugar

12 large egg whites, at room temperature

Pinch of salt

1½ teaspoons cream of tartar

¾ teaspoon vanilla extract

3 cups strawberries, sliced

trisha tip

Important: Don't grease the tube pan, because the batter needs to climb up the sides while baking.

Yes, you can make angel food cake from scratch—and chocolate angel food cake to boot! This recipe is so scrumptious that you might never make it from a mix again. Top with sugared strawberries for a light, sweet finish. I don't need to tell you how good chocolate and strawberries are together. **SERVES 10**

Preheat the oven to 375°F. On a sheet of waxed paper, sift the cake flour with the cocoa and ½ cup of the sugar four times. Using an electric mixer fitted with the whisk attachment, beat the egg whites on high along with a pinch of salt until foamy, about 3 minutes. Sprinkle the cream of tartar over the egg whites and continue beating until they hold a stiff peak, about 5 minutes. Add the vanilla and gradually stream in 1 cup of the remaining sugar.

Using a spatula, gradually fold the flour-sugar mixture into the egg whites, about ¼ cup at a time. Spoon the batter into an ungreased 9-inch tube pan. Bake for 30 minutes, or until a toothpick inserted near the center comes out clean. Remove the pan from the oven, invert, and allow the cake to cool on a rack for 1 hour.

Meanwhile, sprinkle the sliced strawberries with the remaining ¼ cup of sugar. Stir to coat the berries with the sugar and let them stand for about 30 minutes to allow their juices to develop.

hawaiian cake

CAKE

3 cups all-purpose flour

1 teaspoon salt

1 teaspoon baking soda

2 cups sugar

1½ cups vegetable oil

1½ teaspoons vanilla extract

3 large eggs, at room temperature

1 (11-ounce) can mandarin oranges, drained

FROSTING

1 (8-ounce) package cream cheese, softened

¼ cup sour cream

1 (29-ounce) can crushed pineapple, drained

1 cup nondairy topping (I like Cool Whip)

At Hawaiian luaus, home of the original pig in the ground, they serve a cake like this one for dessert. In my family, this cake goes by the informal name of "Pig Pickin' Cake." (The Georgia name for luau is pig pickin'!) This dessert is sweetness personified, with mandarin oranges in the cake and crushed pineapple in the frosting. I didn't think anybody would be too excited about trying to make something called a Pig Pickin' Cake! Aren't you glad I changed the name? **SERVES 12**

Preheat the oven to 350°F. Grease and flour a 9 × 13-inch baking pan and set aside.

Sift the flour, salt, and baking soda into an electric mixer bowl. Add the sugar to the mixing bowl and mix on low until blended. Add the oil, vanilla, and eggs, mixing well. Fold in the mandarin oranges until just incorporated. Pour the batter into the prepared pan and bake for 35 minutes, or until a toothpick inserted into the center comes out clean. Remove from the oven and allow to cool in the pan for 5 minutes, then turn out onto a rack to cool completely, about 20 minutes.

To make the frosting, using an electric mixer, combine the cream cheese, sour cream, pineapple, and nondairy topping until smooth. Frost only the top of the cooled cake and keep refrigerated until ready to serve.

lemon poppy seed cake

CAKE

1 cup (2 sticks) salted butter, softened

2½ cups granulated sugar

6 large eggs, at room temperature

3 cups all-purpose flour

¼ teaspoon baking soda

1 cup sour cream

2 teaspoons vanilla extract

3 tablespoons freshly grated lemon zest

2 tablespoons poppy seeds

1 to 2 tablespoons freshly picked thyme leaves (optional)

GLAZE

1 cup freshly squeezed lemon juice (about 4 large lemons)

1 cup confectioners' sugar (see Trisha Tip, page 207)

Additional thyme leaves for garnish (optional)

My friend Taylor, aka T-Bone, asked me to make her some sort of lemon dessert for her birthday. I love lemon poppy seed muffins, so I made them into this awesome cake with a lemony glaze to die for. It's just moist, citrus-y goodness! The Bundt pan makes for a really pretty presentation.

SERVES 12

Preheat the oven to 350°F. Grease and flour a Bundt pan and set aside.

Using an electric mixer, beat the butter and the granulated sugar together until creamy. Add the eggs, one at a time, beating until just blended after each addition. Sift together the flour and the baking soda. Add the flour mixture to the butter mixture, alternating with the sour cream and beginning and ending with the flour mixture. Add the vanilla, lemon zest, poppy seeds, and thyme leaves (if desired) and beat until fully combined.

Pour the batter into the Bundt pan and bake for 60 to 75 minutes, or until a toothpick inserted near the center comes out clean. Remove from the oven and allow to cool in the pan for 5 minutes, then turn out onto a rack to cool completely, about 20 minutes.

While the cake is still warm, in a small bowl, mix together the lemon juice and confectioners' sugar. Pierce the top of the cake with a fork to create holes, then pour the mixture over the cake on the rack, allowing the glaze to soak in. Garnish with thyme leaves if desired. This cake is great served warm and will keep refrigerated for up to 2 weeks.

key lime cheesecake with raspberry sauce

CRUST
1½ cups fine graham cracker crumbs

¼ cup sugar

¼ cup (½ stick) salted butter, melted

FILLING
4 (8-ounce) packages cream cheese, softened

1 cup sour cream

4 large eggs, room temperature

1¼ cups sugar

1 tablespoon freshly grated lime zest

½ cup Key lime juice (25 small Key limes or 4 large regular limes)

2½ tablespoons cornstarch (see Trisha Tip, page 193)

2 teaspoons vanilla extract

SAUCE
1½ cups frozen raspberries, thawed

¼ cup sugar

1 teaspoon freshly grated lime zest

I do love chocolate, but more often, given the choice, I will go for a citrus dessert. I added zesty lime juice to my classic cheesecake and topped it with fresh raspberry sauce for a satisfying sweet-tart after-dinner dessert. Who wants to squeeze a dozen tiny Key limes? Not me! Look for Nellie & Joe's Famous Key West Lime Juice in your local grocery. It's made in Key West, Florida, it's the bomb, and it saves you all that squeezing! In the tradition of my mama, I serve this rich dessert with a fresh pot of hot coffee. **SERVES 12**

Preheat the oven to 375°F. Spray the bottom of a 10-inch springform pan with cooking spray. Line the bottom with a round of parchment paper, and spray the paper with cooking spray. Place the pan on a sheet of heavy-duty aluminum foil and bring the foil up the sides to enclose the seam of the pan.

To make the crust, in a small mixing bowl, stir together the crumbs, sugar, and melted butter, then press the mixture firmly into the bottom of the springform pan. Set aside.

To make the filling, using an electric mixer, beat the cream cheese and sour cream until smooth and creamy. Add the eggs, one at a time, beating well after each addition. Add the sugar, lime zest, lime juice, cornstarch, and vanilla, and beat until smooth.

Pour the batter into the prepared crust. Put the foil-wrapped pan into a larger pan, then pour about ½ inch of warm water into the larger pan to surround the smaller pan. Bake for

trisha tip

Fresh raspberries are perfectly acceptable for the sauce but lack the moisture of the thawed frozen raspberries. If using fresh, add a couple of tablespoons of water for smooth blending.

1 hour and 15 minutes, or until the top is lightly brown. Turn off the oven and open the door. Allow the cheesecake to stand in the open oven for 1 hour, then cover and refrigerate for at least 2 hours before serving.

Meanwhile, to make the sauce, process the raspberries, sugar, and lime zest in a food processor or blender until smooth. Chill for at least 1 hour before drizzling over the cheesecake and serving.

texas sheet cake with chocolate ganache

CAKE

1 cup (2 sticks)
salted butter

1 cup water

2 cups self-rising flour
(see Trisha Tip,
page 112)

2 cups sugar

2 large eggs, at room
temperature, beaten

1 teaspoon vanilla extract

½ cup Greek yogurt

GANACHE

1 cup (8 ounces)
semisweet chocolate
chips

¾ cup heavy cream

2 tablespoons
light corn syrup

Everybody in the South has a version of this chocolate sheet cake. I can't tell you how many church socials I've been to where I've eaten this fantastic dessert—and it's always good. Most of the ones I've had have a chocolate fudge frosting, but I top mine with an easy chocolate ganache that takes only five minutes to make! Frosting a cake in the pan is the easiest way to get it done. **SERVES 12**

Preheat the oven to 375°F. Grease and flour a 9 × 13-inch sheet cake pan and set aside.

Melt the butter in a large saucepan over medium heat, add 1 cup of water, then increase the heat to high and bring the mixture to a boil. Remove the pan from the heat and whisk in the flour and sugar, mixing well. Stir in the eggs, vanilla, and yogurt.

Pour the batter into the prepared pan and bake for 20 minutes, or until golden on top. Remove the cake from the oven and allow it to cool in the pan, about 20 minutes.

Meanwhile, to make the ganache, place the chocolate chips in a large heatproof bowl. In a medium saucepan set over medium-high heat, bring the cream and corn syrup just barely to a boil. Stir to combine. Pour the cream mixture over the chocolate and allow it to stand for 5 minutes. Then whisk until smooth. Pour the ganache over the cooled cake and, using an offset spatula, cover the cake completely.

kiwi lime pie

CRUST

1 (11-ounce) box vanilla wafers (I like Nilla)

½ cup sugar

½ cup (1 stick) salted butter, melted

FILLING

2 (14-ounce) cans sweetened condensed milk

2 teaspoons freshly grated lime zest

1 cup Key lime juice (12 Key limes or 4 large regular limes)

8 large egg yolks, at room temperature, lightly beaten

4 to 6 kiwis, peeled and sliced thinly

trisha tip

Can't find fresh Key limes? Try Nellie & Joe's Famous Key West Lime Juice. You can find it in your grocery store next to the lemon juice.

I'm picky about my Key lime pie. I like for it to be tart, but not too tart. Somewhere in the middle lies just the right amount of tartness, and I know it when I taste it! I really like the flavor that using vanilla wafers in place of the traditional graham cracker gives the crust, and kiwis are extra sweet, so they help cut some of that famed tartness. Mama's favorite fruit was a good kiwi. I always thought they were just strange-looking little furry things until I topped this pie with them. Now I'm a fan! SERVES 8

Preheat the oven to 350°F. In a food processor, pulse the vanilla wafers into crumbs. Add the sugar and melted butter and pulse until fully combined. Press the mixture firmly into an ungreased 9-inch pie plate. Set aside.

In a medium bowl, whisk together the condensed milk, lime zest, lime juice, and egg yolks. Pour the mixture into the crust. Bake for 30 minutes. (The center will still jiggle.)

Remove from the oven and cool on a rack for 30 minutes. Top with kiwi slices. Cover with plastic wrap and chill in the refrigerator for at least 2 hours before serving.

boston cream pie

FILLING

½ cup sugar

3 tablespoons cornstarch (see Trisha Tip)

½ teaspoon salt

1 large egg + 3 egg yolks, at room temperature

2 cups whole milk

1 teaspoon vanilla extract

CAKE

¼ cup (½ stick) salted butter, at room temperature

⅔ cup sugar

1 large egg, at room temperature

1½ cups cake flour

1½ teaspoons baking powder

¼ teaspoon salt

¾ cup whole milk

1 teaspoon vanilla extract

TOPPING

1 cup heavy cream

1½ cups (12 ounces) semisweet chocolate chips

Boston cream pie was not something my mother made when I was growing up, but once I tasted it at a friend's house, I knew I had to figure out how to make it for myself. I've never understood why it isn't called Boston cream cake, but who am I to question? I just know it's yummy! The custard is rich, but not too sweet, so it keeps this dessert from being overpowering. The chocolate ganache on top is the perfect finish. This recipe really makes more custard than you need for the pie, but I use it all anyway! I like to serve this pie straight out of the refrigerator, because I love it cold. SERVES 8

To make the custard filling, in a medium saucepan off-heat, whisk together the sugar, cornstarch, and salt. Stir in the whole egg and the 3 yolks, and then stir in the milk. Turn the heat on to medium-high, and cook the mixture, uncovered, stirring constantly, until the custard thickens, 12 to 15 minutes. Remove the pan from the heat and stir in the vanilla. Transfer to a bowl, cover with plastic wrap, and refrigerate while you make the cake. Be sure to place the plastic wrap directly onto the custard to prevent a skin from forming.

To make the cake, preheat the oven to 350°F. Spray a 9-inch round cake pan with cooking spray and set aside.

Using an electric mixer, cream the butter and sugar together until fluffy, about 5 minutes. Add the egg and mix until completely combined. Sift together the cake flour, baking powder, and salt. Add the flour mixture to the butter mixture, alternating with the milk and beginning and ending with the flour. Add the vanilla.

Pour the batter into the prepared pan and bake for 30 to 35 minutes, or until a toothpick inserted in the center comes

trisha tip

If you don't have cornstarch, substitute all-purpose flour. One tablespoon cornstarch equals 2 tablespoons flour.

out clean. Remove the cake from the oven and allow to cool in the pan for 10 minutes, then turn out onto a rack to cool completely, about 20 minutes.

To make the chocolate ganache, in a medium saucepan over medium-high heat, bring the cream to a boil, then immediately remove from the heat. Add the chocolate chips to the cream and stir until completely melted.

To assemble, slice the cake layer in half horizontally. Spread the custard filling onto one layer, then top with the second layer of cake. Spread the ganache over the top of the cake, using an offset spatula or the back of a spoon, allowing it to drizzle down the sides. Refrigerate for at least 2 hours before serving. Store covered in the fridge.

mrs. carter's skillet apple pie

1 cup firmly packed light brown sugar

½ cup (1 stick) salted butter, plus 1 tablespoon melted for crust

2 refrigerated rolled pie crusts (I like Pillsbury)

1 (21-ounce) can apple pie filling

2 tablespoons cinnamon sugar

Vanilla ice cream, for serving

My mama was born and raised in Willacoochee, Georgia. I spent a lot of my childhood visiting my grandparents, cousins, and friends in that wonderful town. My mama's maiden name was Paulk, but family included many more than blood relatives. We played with the Tuckers, Granthams, and Carters, and considered them all part of our big family. Some of my fondest memories include get-togethers and potlucks where these great southern ladies prepared the mouthwatering foods that inspired me to cook. I've known Mrs. Helen Carter my whole life. When I asked her for this recipe, she was almost embarrassed to give it to me because she thought it was too simple. That's exactly what I love about it! Garth suggested adding in extra cinnamon sugar . . . smart guy! **SERVES 6**

Preheat the oven to 400°F. Melt the brown sugar and ½ cup of butter in a 9-inch cast-iron skillet over medium heat. Remove the pan from the heat, and cover with one pie crust.

Pour the apple pie filling on top of the crust, sprinkle with 1 tablespoon of the cinnamon sugar, and cover with the second crust. Brush with the 1 tablespoon of melted butter and sprinkle with the remaining cinnamon sugar.

Bake for 30 minutes, or until golden brown. Serve hot, topped with a generous dollop of vanilla ice cream.

Chocolate Chip Cookie Dough Balls (page 204)

cookies, brownies, bars & more

Beth Lunsford's Chocolate Chip Cookies

Baked Apples

Brownie Batter Cookies

Caramel Apples

Chocolate Chip Cookie Dough Balls

Chocolate Marbled Brownies

Glazed Lemon Cookies

No-Bake Peanut Butter Pretzel Squares

Praline Cheesecake Bars

Snappy Pear-Cranberry Crumble

White Chocolate Cranberry Cookies

beth lunsford's chocolate chip cookies

1 cup (2 sticks) unsalted butter, softened (see Trisha Tip, page 28)

1 cup firmly packed light brown sugar

½ cup granulated sugar

2 large eggs, at room temperature

2½ cups all-purpose flour

1 teaspoon baking soda

¼ teaspoon salt

2 teaspoons vanilla extract

1 (12-ounce) bag of chocolate chunks

1 (12-ounce) bag of semisweet chocolate chips

1 (12-ounce) bag of milk chocolate chips

1½ cups finely chopped pecans

I have my own tried-and-true chocolate chip cookie recipe, as do most of us, but I really wanted to share this one with you, because it's full of chocolate . . . semisweet and milk chips, and chocolate chunks. It is the ultimate decadent dessert! These cookies were given to me by one of my dear friends, who was battling cancer at the same time my mama was and who lost the fight shortly after my mom did. I knew Beth my whole life. Her mother was my second grade school teacher, Mrs. Perry, and her sister Julie was my best friend from first grade on. Every time I enjoy these cookies, I think of Beth and smile. **MAKES 2 TO 3 DOZEN COOKIES**

Preheat the oven to 350°F.

Using an electric mixer, cream together the butter and sugars until fluffy. Add the eggs one at a time, mixing after each addition.

In a medium bowl, whisk together the flour, baking soda, and salt. Add the flour mixture to the creamed butter mixture by the spoonful until fully incorporated. Add the vanilla. Fold in all the chocolate chunks and chips and the nuts.

Drop the cookies by generous spoonfuls, 2 inches apart, onto an ungreased cookie sheet. Bake for 10 to 12 minutes until slightly browned around the edges. Remove the baking sheet from the oven, and transfer the cookies to a rack to cool completely, about 10 minutes. Store in an airtight container for up to 2 weeks.

baked apples

4 large baking apples

¼ cup butter (½ stick), softened

½ cup firmly packed light brown sugar

¾ teaspoon cinnamon

¼ cup chopped pecans

2 cinnamon sticks (optional)

trisha tip

It's important to use a type of apple that will hold its shape when baked, so be sure to choose a sturdy baking apple like Granny Smith, Fuji, or Honeycrisp.

One of the joys of fall is fresh apples—Braeburn, Gala, Fuji—I could go on and on! I discovered Honeycrisps last fall and used them in this mouthwatering recipe. Your kitchen will smell like apple-cinnamon heaven! SERVES 4

Preheat the oven to 375°F. Wash and core the apples, leaving ½ inch of the core at the base of the apple to contain the filling.

In a small bowl, combine the butter, brown sugar, cinnamon, and chopped pecans. Spoon enough of the mixture into each apple to fill the core to the top.

Fill a 2-quart glass baking dish with ¾ cup of water. Place the apples upright in the dish. Lay the cinnamon sticks in the water. Bake until the apples are soft and the filling is browned, about 1 hour. Serve plain or top with ice cream or whipped topping.

brownie batter cookies

1 cup (2 sticks) salted butter, softened

1 ounce unsweetened baking chocolate, melted

1¼ cups granulated sugar

¾ cup firmly packed dark brown sugar

3 large eggs, at room temperature

2½ cups all-purpose flour

½ cup unsweetened cocoa powder

1¼ teaspoons salt

1¼ teaspoons baking powder

1 tablespoon vanilla extract

1½ cups semisweet chocolate chips

It seems like my friends and I are always thinking up ways to combine our favorite foods into one recipe! These cookies were the result of one of those, "Hey, what if . . ." conversations. I mixed my favorite chocolate chip cookie dough with my mama's classic brownie recipe, and the result is beyond heavenly. **MAKES 3 DOZEN COOKIES**

Preheat the oven to 350°F. Line a large baking sheet with parchment paper and set aside.

Using an electric mixer fitted with the paddle attachment, beat the butter, chocolate, and sugars until smooth. Add the eggs, one at a time, mixing well after each addition.

On a sheet of waxed paper, sift together the flour, cocoa powder, salt, and baking powder and add slowly into the butter mixture until smooth. Add the vanilla and fold in the chocolate chips.

Drop the cookies by heaping tablespoonfuls onto the prepared baking sheet, about 2 inches apart. Bake for 12 to 15 minutes, or until just browned around the edges, but still soft in the center. Remove the baking sheet from the oven and transfer the cookies to a rack to cool completely, about 10 minutes.

caramel apples

10 medium Granny Smith apples

10 popsicle sticks or chopsticks

Crushed toppings of your choice (I like Oreos)

2 cups sugar

1 cup buttermilk (see Trisha Tip)

½ cup (1 stick) salted butter

1 teaspoon baking soda

1 teaspoon vanilla extract

Heavy cream, to thin the caramel, if necessary

Sea salt

1 (12-ounce) bag white chocolate chips

Mama always made red candy apples for us when we were children, and I loved them, but they were so hard to eat! After I grew up and started making them for my own children, I cut the apples into pieces before dipping them into the red candy coating to make eating them a little easier. When I discovered caramel apples, I was in heaven. I love caramel-covered anything, so these were right up my alley. What I especially like about using Granny Smith apples is that they are tart and cut some of the supersweetness of the caramel. They are also a gorgeous lime green, so they make a beautiful treat. These apples are best eaten the same day you make them, but you won't have any left over anyway! **MAKES 10 CARAMEL APPLES**

trisha tip

Adding 1 tablespoon vinegar to 1 cup milk makes 1 cup buttermilk. You can use a different acidic component like lemon juice for the same effect. Use this tip when a recipe calls for buttermilk and you don't have any on hand.

Rinse and dry the apples. Spray a baking sheet with cooking spray. Push one stick into the bottom of each apple, then place apple on the baking sheet with the stick standing straight up.

Place the toppings in a large sealable plastic bag and roll with a rolling pin to crush. Set aside.

In a large saucepan over low heat, combine the sugar, buttermilk, butter, baking soda, and vanilla and bring just to a boil, stirring constantly. Attach a candy thermometer to the pan, and continue to boil and stir until the mixture reaches 238°F, 15 to 17 minutes. Remove the pan from the heat.

Dip each apple, one at a time, immediately into the caramel, leaving a ¼-inch ring of green by the stick, and return the apple to the baking sheet. If the caramel starts to solidify while you are dipping apples, stir in heavy cream, a few drops at a time, until the caramel reaches a spreadable consistency.

After all the apples have been dipped, lightly sprinkle them with sea salt. Allow the caramel to set, about 5 minutes.

Meanwhile, in a microwave-safe bowl, microwave the white chocolate chips on high in 30-second intervals, stirring until melted. Dip each apple into the melted white chocolate, leaving a ¼-inch ring of caramel exposed. Immediately dip the white chocolate–covered caramel apple in a layer of crushed toppings, leaving ¼ inch of the white chocolate exposed.

*Bret on Halloween
(2005).*

*Beth and me on Halloween
(1968).*

chocolate chip cookie dough balls

BALLS

⅔ cup (1⅓ sticks) salted butter, softened

¾ cup granulated sugar

¼ cup firmly packed light brown sugar

¼ cup applesauce

1 teaspoon vanilla extract

1¾ cups sifted all-purpose flour

½ teaspoon baking soda

½ teaspoon salt

1 cup mini semisweet chocolate chips

DIPPING CHOCOLATE

6 ounces dark chocolate wafers

3 blocks (5.25 ounces) chocolate almond bark or CandyQuik

trisha tip

To make white chocolate dip, use 6 ounces white chocolate chips and 3 blocks (5.25 ounces) of vanilla almond bark.

I don't know anybody who doesn't eat raw cookie dough. I used to buy those pre-packaged frozen Mrs. GoodCookie chocolate chip cookies and eat the dough before I could ever get them in the oven! Ditto for making homemade chocolate chip cookies. But every time I eat raw dough, I hear my mother's voice in my head saying, "Don't eat that! It has raw egg in it!" Didn't we all eat the raw egg? Rocky did, and he turned out okay! Anyway, I substituted applesauce for the egg here. In cookies, the egg's function is usually for binding, so applesauce is a great substitute. It does the job, and then you can eat all the raw dough you want. Of course, I dip these in chocolate just to make them more fancy, but they're just as good plain! **MAKES 3 TO 4 DOZEN COOKIE BALLS**

Using an electric mixer, beat together the butter, sugars, applesauce, and vanilla until smooth. In a medium bowl, whisk together the flour, baking soda, and salt. With the beater running on low, slowly add the dry ingredients to the butter mixture. Stir in the chocolate chips.

Using a mini ice cream scoop, scoop out the batter and roll into balls, about 1 inch in diameter. Place the dough balls about 1 inch apart on an ungreased cookie sheet. Put the cookie sheet in the freezer and allow the dough to set, about 30 minutes.

Meanwhile, in a medium microwave-safe bowl, microwave the chocolate wafers and the almond bark together on high in 30-second intervals until melted, stirring between each interval.

Remove the chilled dough balls from the freezer, and using two spoons or forks, dip the dough balls into the chocolate, then place onto parchment or waxed paper. Store in a tightly covered container in the refrigerator for up to 3 weeks.

chocolate marbled brownies

1 tablespoon unsalted butter (softened for greasing)

1 cup (2 sticks) unsalted butter (see Trisha Tip, page 28)

6 ounces bittersweet chocolate, chopped

½ cup unsweetened cocoa powder

2 cups granulated sugar

½ teaspoon salt

1⅓ cups all-purpose flour

3 large eggs, at room temperature

1 (8-ounce) package cream cheese, softened

½ cup confectioners' sugar (see Trisha Tip)

½ teaspoon vanilla extract

You can never go wrong with brownies and cream cheese! I adore all things "brownie," from Betty Crocker's quick and easy boxed mix to Mama's homemade classics. It's all good! I love the silkiness that the cream cheese swirl brings to this dessert, and they're so beautiful. These brownies are the perfect elegant treat to take to a party or bake sale.

MAKES 9 BROWNIES

Preheat the oven to 325°F. Grease a 9 × 9-inch baking dish with the softened butter and set aside.

In a medium saucepan over medium-low heat, melt the 1 cup of butter and chocolate together, stirring constantly, until smooth. Remove the pan from the heat and stir in the cocoa powder, granulated sugar, salt, flour, and 2 of the eggs. Pour the batter into the prepared dish.

Using an electric mixer, beat the cream cheese until smooth, 3 to 4 minutes. Add the confectioners' sugar, vanilla, and the remaining egg. Mix until smooth. Dollop the cream cheese mixture over the top of the brownie batter. Using a butter knife or fork, swirl the mixtures together to form a design.

Bake for 45 to 50 minutes, or until the brownies just slightly pull away from sides of the baking dish. Remove from the oven and allow to cool in the pan for 15 minutes. Slice into 9 squares and serve.

trisha tip

You can make your own confectioners' sugar by streaming granulated sugar into the small opening of a blender set at high speed. One cup of granulated sugar makes ¾ cup of confectioners'.

glazed lemon cookies

COOKIES

¾ cup (1½ sticks) salted butter, softened

¾ cup granulated sugar

2 large egg yolks, at room temperature

½ teaspoon vanilla extract

2 teaspoons freshly grated lemon zest (about 1 medium lemon)

2 cups all-purpose flour

GLAZE

1 cup confectioners' sugar (see Trisha Tip, page 207)

1 teaspoon freshly grated lemon zest

2 tablespoons freshly squeezed lemon juice

trisha tip

After whisking together the glaze, pour it out onto a salad plate or a small bowl to make dipping the cookies easier, or brush the glaze on with a pastry brush.

I have to confess that although I bake everything from cakes to pies to cookies to candy, my frosting of said baked goods is not always the most attractive. I always say that my cakes taste really good, but they might not be pretty enough for a bake sale! There is definitely an art to frosting, but glazing is much easier. These are my go-to if I ever need to take a dessert to a party or event. The glaze sets so nicely, you'd almost think they came from a bakery. Almost! **MAKES 4 TO 5 DOZEN COOKIES**

Preheat the oven to 350°F. Line 2 baking sheets with parchment paper and set aside.

Using an electric mixer, beat the butter and granulated sugar until the mixture is light and fluffy. Add the egg yolks, vanilla, and zest, and beat until combined. Add the flour to the mixture, a little at a time, until a soft dough forms.

Divide the dough in half and, using your hands, shape it into 2 logs, each 2 inches in diameter. Wrap the logs in waxed paper and refrigerate until firm, about 30 minutes. Cut the logs into ¼-inch-thick slices and place them on the baking sheets about 2 inches apart.

Bake the cookies for 15 to 18 minutes, or until the edges are slightly browned. Remove from the oven and allow to cool on the baking sheets for 10 minutes.

Meanwhile, in a small bowl, whisk together the confectioners' sugar and the lemon zest and juice. Dip the top of each cookie into the glaze, and place the cookies on a cooling rack set over the baking sheets. Allow to set for about 15 minutes before serving. Store in an airtight container for up to 2 weeks.

no-bake peanut butter pretzel squares

2 cups thin pretzel sticks

¾ cup (1½ sticks) salted butter, melted

1½ cups confectioners' sugar (see Trisha Tip, page 207)

1¼ cups smooth peanut butter

1½ cups milk chocolate chips

trisha tip

Thin pretzel sticks have the perfect amount of crunch and salt for the bottom layer.

Everyone loves Reese's Peanut Butter Cups, right? If you don't like them, I really just can't know you! Most no-bake "Reese's" cups use crushed graham crackers in the bottom crust, but I use pretzel crumbs. The salt and the crunch send this treat over the top! The best part is that they only take about five minutes to put together. The hard part is waiting the thirty minutes for them to get cold enough to slice! **MAKES 16 SQUARES**

In a food processor, pulse the pretzels into fine crumbs, about 2 minutes. In a medium bowl, mix together the pretzel crumbs, melted butter, confectioners' sugar, and 1 cup of the peanut butter until fully combined. Press evenly into the bottom of an ungreased 9 × 9-inch pan.

In a medium microwave safe bowl, melt the remaining ¼ cup of peanut butter and the chocolate chips together in 30-second intervals, stirring in between. When the mixture is smooth, spread it over the peanut butter–pretzel layer. Refrigerate for at least 30 minutes before cutting into squares.

praline cheesecake bars

1 cup graham cracker crumbs

3 tablespoons granulated sugar

3 tablespoons salted butter, melted

3 (8-ounce) packages cream cheese, softened

1 cup firmly packed dark brown sugar

2 tablespoons all-purpose flour

3 large eggs, at room temperature

1½ teaspoons vanilla extract

½ cup finely chopped pecans

The story is that "long ago and far away," French settlers brought to New Orleans the praline, an amazing confection made from brown sugar, cream, and pecans. My family has always enjoyed Savannah's River Street Sweets version— and thought pralines mixed with cheesecake could be a sweet dream! They make great treats to take to a party. Whether you pronounce it "prah-lean" or "pray-lean," they're just plain good! **MAKES 9 BARS**

Preheat the oven to 350°F. Line the bottom of a 9 × 9-inch square pan with parchment paper, spray with cooking spray, and set aside.

In a medium bowl, combine the crumbs, granulated sugar, and melted butter, and press into the bottom of the prepared pan. Bake until browned, 8 to 10 minutes. Remove from the oven, and set aside.

Increase the oven temperature up to 450°F, and make the filling. Using an electric mixer, beat the cream cheese until fluffy, then add the brown sugar and flour. Add the eggs one at a time, beating well after each addition. Add the vanilla. Fold in the chopped pecans.

Pour the batter into the crust and bake for 10 minutes. Reduce the oven temperature to 250°F and bake for an additional 50 minutes, or until slightly browned on top. Remove from the oven, and allow to cool completely, about 20 minutes, then refrigerate for at least 2 hours. Cut into 9 bars before serving.

snappy pear-cranberry crumble

CRUMBLE

1 cup all-purpose flour

¼ cup granulated sugar

¼ cup firmly packed brown sugar

1 cup gingersnap cookie crumbs (16 to 18 finely crushed cookies)

¼ teaspoon salt

½ cup (1 stick) salted butter, melted

FILLING

2 pounds (4 to 5 large) pears, peeled, cored, and sliced crosswise ¼ inch thick

¾ cup dried cranberries, chopped

1 teaspoon freshly grated orange zest

1 tablespoon freshly squeezed orange juice

½ teaspoon vanilla extract

½ cup granulated sugar

2 tablespoons cornstarch (see Trisha Tip, page 193)

My sister Beth made this dish for the first time when she and her family were invited to share Thanksgiving with a neighbor's family. She knew that there would be a houseful of good cooks, so she didn't want to make something to "compete" with a favorite pie or cake. This fall dish mingles pears, cranberries, and orange zest with a gingersnap crumb topping that was a big hit at the dessert table. Thank goodness! SERVES 8

Preheat the oven to 350°F. Brush a 2-quart baking dish with softened butter and set aside.

To make the crumble, in a large bowl, mix together the flour, sugars, crumbs, and salt. Stir in the melted butter until crumbles form. Set aside.

To make the filling, in a separate bowl, mix together the pear slices, cranberries, orange zest and juice, vanilla, granulated sugar, and cornstarch.

Pour into the prepared baking dish, and sprinkle the gingersnap crumble over the top. Bake for 40 to 45 minutes, or until golden brown and bubbly. Remove from the oven and allow to cool for 10 minutes. Serve warm.

white chocolate cranberry cookies

½ cup (1 stick) salted butter, softened

½ cup firmly packed light brown sugar

½ cup granulated sugar

¼ cup unsweetened applesauce

1 tablespoon vanilla extract

1½ cups all-purpose flour

1½ teaspoons baking soda

1 cup white chocolate chips

¾ cup dried cranberries, chopped

1 cup macadamia nuts, chopped

¾ cup fresh frozen coconut, thawed (optional)

These cookies combine everything I love about dessert: white chocolate, cranberries, and macadamia nuts . . . oh, my! Garth loves coconut, so I add it in when baking these for him. I started making these treats for our annual Christmas cookie party a few years ago, and they have become a favorite to eat and give away as gifts for the holidays. Of course, we try not to eat more than we give away! **MAKES 2 DOZEN COOKIES**

Preheat the oven to 350°F. Line a baking sheet with parchment paper and set aside.

Using an electric mixer fitted with the paddle attachment, cream the butter and sugars together until light and fluffy. Add the applesauce and vanilla, mixing well.

In a medium bowl, whisk together the flour and baking soda. With the mixer on low, spoon the flour mixture gradually into the creamed sugar mixture. Fold in the white chocolate chips, cranberries, macadamia nuts, and coconut (if using).

Drop the cookies by heaping spoonfuls onto the prepared baking sheet, about 2 inches apart. Bake for 10 to 12 minutes, or until the edges are browned. Remove the baking sheet from the oven and transfer the cookies to a rack to cool, about 10 minutes. Store in an airtight container for up to 2 weeks.

equipment favorites

In a lot of my recipes I've suggested pan sizes, ingredient substitutions, information sources, and the like. The following list includes my must-haves in the kitchen and why they're my go-to items.

CAST-IRON SKILLET: A skillet (9 or 10 inches in diameter) is most useful. I am lucky to have one of my mama's cast-iron skillets, seasoned with love from years of cooking for our family. If you buy a new skillet, you'll need to season it before using. Here's how: Coat the inside of the skillet with vegetable shortening (not butter) and heat in a 450°F oven for 1 hour. Remove from the oven, cool the skillet, and wipe off any excess oil before using. To care for a seasoned skillet, wipe the interior with a paper towel after each use. Never soak it in soapy water or put it in the dishwasher.

BAKING SHEETS: Be sure you have at least two high-quality baking sheets that fit in your oven. Nonstick cookie sheets are usually darker, and they bake a browner, crispier cookie (especially on the bottom) more quickly than a light, shiny sheet. To make softer cookies, an insulated cookie sheet works best, but note that they are not dishwasher safe.

JELLY ROLL PAN: I call this a cookie sheet with sides! Jelly roll pans or rimmed baking sheets have low sides, usually ½ to 1 inch deep. I use these pans for any recipe that has juicy drippings. They can also be used for baking cookies, biscuits, or jelly rolls, of course! Have at least two.

MEASURING SPOONS: I like to have at least three sets of measuring spoons. Make sure to get a set that can be separated so you don't have to wash all the spoons when you just use one! I like using either plastic or metal spoons.

MEASURING CUPS: Two sets for dry measuring and two sets for liquid measuring. There is a difference! With dry measuring cups, you fill right up to the top and then level off with a flat-edged knife or spatula. Liquid measuring cups usually have a pour spout and should be filled according to the markings on the side of the cup. I love the OXO brand liquid measures because you can see the markings from the top. They're so easy to read!

ELECTRIC STAND MIXER: My mixer of choice is a KitchenAid with attachments that include a flat beater, a wire whip, a dough hook, and a grater. There are tons more attachments available, from food grinders to pasta makers! I recommend buying an extra mixer bowl for those days when you're whipping up mashed potatoes and putting together a cake batter. If I had to pick one appliance to spring for in my kitchen, it would be an electric mixer. It's my go-to gift for brides and grooms.

HEAVY-DUTY BLENDER: I bought a Vitamix a few years ago and did away with my regular blender altogether. It does the small jobs like late-night milkshakes, but it also handles the bigger jobs like making fresh cashew cream or pureeing soups. The powerful motor saves the step of straining

through a sieve, and to clean the pitcher, you simply add a little dishwashing liquid to about an inch of warm water, put the lid on, and blend on high for a few seconds. Rinse it out, and you're ready to use it again.

SLOW COOKER: I like a large (at least 4 to 5 quarts) slow cooker. They are ideal for soup, chili, stew, and meats that can cook all day while you get other things done. I suggest buying one with a removable liner. It works great as a serving dish and makes cleanup easier.

PRESSURE COOKER: A 4- to 6-quart pressure cooker speeds up cooking for our busy lives. I recently switched from the traditional stovetop pressure cooker to an electric version, and I love it. It's efficient and doubles as a slow cooker if I need an extra one. A good pressure cooker greatly reduces your cook time in the kitchen. Cook potatoes for 5 minutes instead of boiling for 30. Chicken breasts cook in 10 to 15 minutes instead of 45. Who wouldn't like that?

FOOD PROCESSOR: I use a big 14-cup Cuisinart processor, even for the smaller jobs. It's super versatile! I use mine for chopping nuts, pureeing the perfect pesto, and for making creamy dips and spreads. It will even chop cooked meats for salads or soups.

thanks

Putting together a cookbook takes so many people, and this one is no exception. Thanks to everyone at my publishing home, Clarkson Potter, especially Pam Krauss, Aaron Wehner, Doris Cooper, Amanda Englander, Patricia Shaw, Mary Anne Stewart, Luisa Francavilla, Rae Ann Spitzenberger, Michael Nagin, Meredith McGinnis, and Kate Tyler. Thank you for helping me continue to feed my passion for cooking. To Team Trisha: Ken Levitan and Michelle Owens at Vector Management, David Vigliano, Paula Breen, the gang at WME Entertainment, and Rusty Jones, Tiffany Shipp, Cheryl Harris, Dana Dennis, Aris Schwab, and O'Neil Hagaman. Thank you for the never-ending adventure that is my career!

The third time is a charm, and Ben Fink, your photographs are exquisite, only equaled by your gentle nature and loving personality. I adore you. Special thanks to Joe Tully, Jeff Kavanaugh, Dennis O'Clair, Angie Moser, Libbie Summers, Candace Bower, Rachel Cleary, Ali Beckett, Ellen Summers, Raven King, and Joel Hood for assisting, preparing, and documenting everything necessary for the shoots in New York and Nashville. Thank you to Perry Hagopian for shooting the cookbook cover. Thank you for your friendship and your talent! Thanks to Katie Maco, Lindsey Sherman, Erin Turon, Caroline Ward, Titilayo Bankole, Jen Everett, and Anthony Moschini for assisting on the shoot.

Thanks to Earl Cox, Mary Beth Felts, Claudia Fowler, and Callie Blackburn for hair, makeup, wardrobe, and laughter. You make the Yearwood family shine!

Melissa Perry, your sense of humor helps me handle the long hours! Thank you for testing these recipes and helping me develop some new ones. Thanks for all the late-night chats and food photos. I love you dearly. Special thanks to Jenny Bierman, Christina Wu, Morgan Hass, and Mary Beth Bray for being the culinary queens that you are.

Thank you to the family and friends who contributed recipes and photos for this book: Jan Anderson, Jana Brooks, Jan Burton, Helen Carter, Julie Colbert, Kelli Ferner, Billie Jo Flanagan, Lauren Fresh, Ann Fundis, Lory Garcia, Shirley Anne Gilliam, Benita Hill, Donna Holbrook, Hope Kozma, Isabelle LaChimia, Jimmy and Beth Lunsford, Shari Mackaye, Donna Powell, Tal Ronnen, Gail Shoup, Guy Thomson, and Karri Turner. Thank you for your friendship and generosity.

A big thank-you to our immediate families: John, Ashley, Kyle, and Bret Bernard, and Garth, Taylor, August, and Allie Brooks. Thanks once again for your patience while it seemed we spent more time writing about food than cooking it and for being our ultimate testers. We love you more than we can say.

Finally, to Beth: Thank you for helping me once again turn a handful of recipes into a beautiful representation of our family. Your encouragement, faith in me, and love of our family always gets me through, whether we're writing a cookbook or enjoying a conversation over coffee. You're my person. I love you.

Trisha

index